T0214454

Cultural Synergy in Information Institutions

Richard P. Smiraglia

Cultural Synergy in Information Institutions

 Springer

Richard P. Smiraglia
University of Wisconsin-Milwaukee
Milwaukee
Wisconsin
USA

ISBN 978-1-4939-5468-1   ISBN 978-1-4939-1249-0 (eBook)
DOI 10.1007/978-1-4939-1249-0
Springer New York Heidelberg Dordrecht London

© Springer Science+Business Media New York 2014
Softcover reprint of the hardcover 1st edition 2014
This work is subject to copyright. All rights are reserved by the Publisher, whether the whole or part of the material is concerned, specifically the rights of translation, reprinting, reuse of illustrations, recitation, broadcasting, reproduction on microfilms or in any other physical way, and transmission or information storage and retrieval, electronic adaptation, computer software, or by similar or dissimilar methodology now known or hereafter developed. Exempted from this legal reservation are brief excerpts in connection with reviews or scholarly analysis or material supplied specifically for the purpose of being entered and executed on a computer system, for exclusive use by the purchaser of the work. Duplication of this publication or parts thereof is permitted only under the provisions of the Copyright Law of the Publisher's location, in its current version, and permission for use must always be obtained from Springer. Permissions for use may be obtained through RightsLink at the Copyright Clearance Center. Violations are liable to prosecution under the respective Copyright Law.
The use of general descriptive names, registered names, trademarks, service marks, etc. in this publication does not imply, even in the absence of a specific statement, that such names are exempt from the relevant protective laws and regulations and therefore free for general use.
While the advice and information in this book are believed to be true and accurate at the date of publication, neither the authors nor the editors nor the publisher can accept any legal responsibility for any errors or omissions that may be made. The publisher makes no warranty, express or implied, with respect to the material contained herein.

Printed on acid-free paper

Springer is part of Springer Science+Business Media (www.springer.com)

Contents

Chapter 1
Cultural Synergy and the Role of Information Institutions

Abstract Cultural forces govern a synergistic relationship among information institutions that shapes their roles collectively and individually. Cultural synergy is the combination of perception- and behavior-shaping knowledge within, between, and among groups that contributes to the virtual reality of a common information-sharing interface among information institutions. Our hyperlinked era makes information-sharing among institutions critically important for scholarship as well as for the advancement of humankind. Information institutions are those that have, or share in, the mission to preserve, conserve, and disseminate information objects and their informative content. A central idea is the notion of social epistemology—that information institutions arise culturally from social forces of the cultures they inhabit, and that their purpose is to disseminate that culture. All information institutions are alike in critical ways. Intersecting lines of cultural mission are trajectories for synergy—for allowing us to perceive the universe of information institutions as interconnected and evolving and moving forward in distinct ways for the improvement of the condition of humankind through the building up of its knowledge base and of its information-sharing processes.

This book is about the synergistic relationship—both real and virtual—among institutions that preserve, conserve, and disseminate information objects and their informative content. A central thesis of this book is not that there is such a synergistic relationship—we take that as a given. Rather, a central thesis is that cultural forces govern the synergistic relationship among information institutions and thus shapes their roles collectively and individually. Synergy is that combination of forces whose power is greater than the individual power of its constituent elements. Culture is that base of knowledge that is common to any particular group of people, such that it shapes their perception as well as their behavior as a group and as members of that group. Cultural synergy, then, is the combination of perception- and behavior-shaping knowledge within, between, and among groups that contributes to the now realized virtual reality of a common information-sharing interface among information institutions.

In this book I explore the cultural synergy that can be realized by seeing commonalities among information institutions—sometimes, interestingly, also called cultural heritage institutions—primarily museums, libraries and archives. But I also take the opportunity to broaden the notion of information institution to embrace the powerful institutions that govern the acquisition and ordering of knowledge, as well

R. P. Smiraglia, *Cultural Synergy in Information Institutions,*
DOI 10.1007/978-1-4939-1249-0_1, © Springer Science+Business Media New York 2014

as those that now seem to encompass our increasingly virtual social lives. All of these are information institutions; all of them can be part of synergistic advances in shaping perception of knowledge that serves as a form of social capital in our hyperlinked era. The oft-promised Semantic Web, if it arrives, will make information-sharing among institutions critically important not only for scholarship but also for the advancement of humankind. This book contains a series of short essays in which I address the origins of cultural heritage information institutions, the history of the professions that manage them, and the social imperative of knowledge organization as a catalyst for cultural information synergy.

1.1 About Commonality of Information Institutions

Information institutions are those that have, or share in, the mission to preserve, conserve, and disseminate information objects and their informative content. We think of institutions, often, as associated with their physical presences—usually in the form of great buildings or campuses. But an institution is more than its housing. It is an organization, perhaps even a sort of organism, in which all of the parts work together even in often inordinately discrete roles, not only to achieve a common goal but also to contribute to the vitality and therefore the ongoing life of the central institution. This quality is shared by all manner of institutions, from central banks to supreme courts to universities and so on. Information institutions frequently are described as systems—a system is a series of discrete functions that aid or impede one another—information institutions have inputs, outputs, and internal communications that keep them functioning. An essential aspect of any system is ongoing unimpeded communication among the components. If at any point communication breaks down, the whole system fails.

Our information institutions involve the dissemination of the knowledge held by a culture, which means that acquiring, maintaining and disseminating artifacts of knowledge are the primary functions of the system. Here is a diagram of such a system:

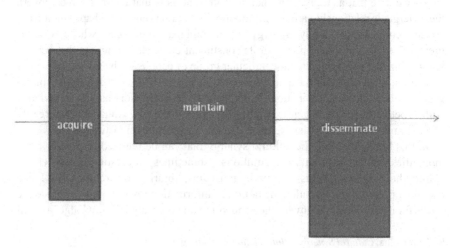

This is a pretty simple system. It has three discrete components: acquisiton, maintenance, and dissemination, and it has a line that stretches through all three to represent communication. If any of the three components or the communication channel
break down, the system will fail. Of course, our institutions are quite a lot more
complex than this. Acquisition requires domain knowledge (subject expertise), understanding of the marketplace, and the relationship of one collection to all others.
Maintenance requires some sort of inventory control, and some sort of preservation
action. Dissemination requires an interfacing query system, a loan or exhibit system
(or both), as well as a system for public interface. Each of these, for instance, can
be seen as a system as well. Sometimes the boundaries overlap. For instance, in
most libraries, there is a "technical services" division responsible for everything
except public interface. That means acquisitions, cataloging, system maintenance
(the computer systems), circulation, and even preservation, are all seen as components of our central "maintenance" block. But as you can see, the whole system is
dependent on the functioning of the whole of "technical services." So what happens
when we add users with queries? Then we have a true information system:

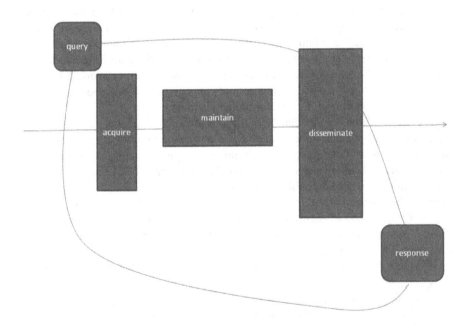

Query and response are in an infinite loop that circulates around the whole system,
to illustrate the central role of the human information interface. People have problems; they require the cultural resources of our institutions to help solve them. But
it is an ongoing interface that surrounds everything we do. And there is communica-

tion not only within our system and not only between the query and response in the human system, but between these two components as well.

Institutions also, usually, share a certain core of what has come to be called *gravitas*, which simply means they are important and usually somber as it pertains to their social roles and their perceived importance in their communities. Churches and libraries both come to mind as excellent examples of institutions with (buildings, and) a keen sense of *gravitas*. Less obvious examples include digital services such as *WebDewey*, the *Naxos Music Library*, and social networking loci such as *Facebook* and *Twitter*.

We can try to enumerate the sorts of institutions that have as their central role the mission to preserve, conserve, and disseminate information objects and their informative content. These are, as we already have said, museums, archives, and libraries, of course. But there are more kinds of information institutions. There are information centers, information corporations, and even large knowledge organization systems that all can certainly fall under the moniker of information institution. The Bata Shoe Museum, The Bibliothéque Nationale de France, and the Archives of American Art are all information institutions. But so are the Finnish Music Information Centre, the Web of Knowledge™, and the *Dewey Decimal Classification*. In every case, a large organization employs many participants in diverse roles working in sync toward the common goal of preserving, conserving and disseminating information objects and their informative content. Each of the six information institutions named here as examples holds a position of respect, or *gravitas* in their communities and beyond, and each is not only engaged in its core mission but also in the preservation of itself as an information institution.

The thesis of this book is that there is more to the commonality of information institutions, that perhaps it has something to do with their cultural roots, because their cultural roots determine their cultural life-support systems. We have stated rather simply that culture is that base of knowledge common to any group of people. That definition is accurate and simple; but its meaning is diverse and complex. What is the culture of The Bata Shoe Museum? Canada? Toronto? The University of Toronto? The Museum locale near the capital of Ontario? North America? Shoes? Western culture? All culture? What is the cultural base of this information institution? Well, we cannot determine that without asking the institution itself. On its website it says (http://www.batashoemuseum.ca/about/unique_museum.shtml):

> Discover the treasures of North America's charming and surprising shoe museum. Hundreds of shoes (from a collection numbering over 10,000) are on exhibit in architect Raymond Moriyama's award-winning four-storey structure. The Museum celebrates the style and function of footwear …. Footwear on display ranges from Chinese bound foot shoes and ancient Egyptian sandals to chestnut-crushing clogs and glamourous platforms. Over 4,500 years of history and a collection of 20th-century celebrity shoes are reflected in the semi-permanent exhibition, *All About Shoes*.

So the culture is "North American" and yet international, the culture is about shoes but as informative objects. Furthermore, at the top of the website the museum identifies itself as "for the curious." And yet that, too, is indeterminate.

What does it mean to say that information institutions are subject to cultural synergy? It means simply that every information institution springs from within a culture, and therefore represents that culture from which it has sprung, but also can be found in alignment with other aligning cultures. That long list above is correct: the Bata Shoe Museum is Canadian, Ontarian, Shoe-centric, Feminist, Western, (but because it is Canadian it also is) multi-cultural. And that means that it has, therefore, not a single cultural mission but many. It is the overlapping and enrichment of these circles of cultural synergy that demonstrate true synergy is taking place. That is, this is how we know that cultural institutions are more than the sum of the list of them. And thus we see the complexity of an institutional organism, but also the richness of the synergy of all of them.

The final point of commonality is the mundane daily function of such institutions. To loan books or paintings or sculptures, to buy statues or artifacts or digital files, to expand the schedule of a classification. These are the functions by which information institutions carry out their complex missions. And in this there is major harmony, which is an opening for synergy. Do museums catalog artifacts in the same way libraries catalog books? No, but maybe. That is, object cataloging in a museum is a more complex task descriptively and archeologically than entering a book into a short bibliographical record. But, the library, in the museum archives, probably has used standard library practice to catalog the artifact and anything written about it. Here is a literal synergy—the information action of two different information institutions acting on the same information object. Let us look more closely at how his might be done.

1.2 About Social Epistemology and Cultural Imperatives

I already have stated that my central thesis is that cultural forces govern the synergistic relationship among information institutions and that this synergy shapes the collective or virtual roles of the institutions in society. This thesis is based on a theory that emerged from mid-twentieth century library-and-information science that often is attributed to Jesse Hauk Shera, although recently it has been more properly attributed to his colleague Margaret Egan (Furner 2004). This theory is called "social epistemology" and it will inform a line of thought throughout this text, and the core of Chap. 6 where information dissemination is treated directly. For now, let us simply state the idea as clearly as possible in an elementary way. Epistemology is the science of knowledge, rooted traditionally in philosophy, which tells us how it is that we know what we know. In knowledge organization and information science, epistemology is used to define what we call domains, or communities with a common knowledge base—such as disciplines like medicine or music, or even work-centric communities such as an individual human relations firm. In any event, a common epistemology derives from the method of knowing that the group employs. A typical kind of epistemology is empirical, that is, that which we know from perceived experience. If I walk out the door and water falls on my head, I have empirical knowledge about water falling. With the use of continued stepwise experimentation I might even discover that it is raining (rather than, say, that my neighbor is washing the front of his house with a garden hose). This knowledge is empirical because it is the result of perceived reality in our own real-time experience. Other approaches to epistemology (such as rationalism or pragmatism) involve different approaches to experience. The most often cited paper on epistemology in the information domain is Hjørland (1998); a more recent paper is my own (Smiraglia 2012).

Social epistemology is a formulation that comes from within the information domain (again many cite Shera, e.g. 1965; but more recent reviews are Furner 2002, 2004) and thus is based on perceptions of the social roles of information and the institutions that preserve, conserve and disseminate it. Simply put, the notion of social epistemology is that information institutions arise culturally from social forces of the cultures they inhabit, and that their purpose is to disseminate that culture. This means first that information institutions arise naturally within their cultures. For example, my earliest experiences with music libraries were all in school music department offices. Frustrated by trying to make use of the limited offerings of the school library, many music departments began setting aside a shelf or two for music or recordings of common interest. Before long these collections grew along with the curriculum and the diverse needs of an ever-changing student body. Eventually this very pragmatic collection had become "the music library"—completely a creation of the domain, and as well a creature (or living member) of the domain. In this way the "music library" per se had arisen naturally within the culture of the school music department. Along the way the missions of collecting, preserving and conserving, and circulating joined together to become the collective mission of disseminating the culture of the individual department. Similarly, an undergraduate geology department of my acquaintance had its own room full of rocks—a "museum" as it were, arising from the culture. These are simplistic examples, but we can see already how easily this model applies to all information institutions. Not only can we apply the model in retrospect, but we can see that it is a naturalistic explanation of how such institutions always have evolved across time. It is another piece of the puzzle of our central thesis. Cultural prerogatives shape information institutions, and they all share that characteristic, and this can be seen as a synergistic force.

1.2.1 Of Information, Sharing, and Information Institutions

Of course, another thing shared by all information institutions is information itself. There are many different approaches to the definition of information in competition in the scholarship in general and in the information domain in particular. That discussion forms the core of Chap. 2, and its thread will extend through the rest of this book. So once again I defer arguments here by stating briefly that throughout this book I am using the definition of information as the process of becoming informed. That means that knowledge (or, data, for example) is potential information waiting to be communicated (or shared) across space and time to receivers for whom its perception will be part of a process.

A simple example is the internal temperature pork should reach before being safe to be served as food—the datum, or the bit of recorded knowledge, is that a thermometer inserted into the pork should reach a temperature of 145 °F/63 °C before removing the meat from the heat (the temperature will continue to rise after cooking for a few minutes). Is this information? The answer (by my definition) is no, not as a simple datum. But, when a host preparing a crown roast of pork for Christmas dinner consults the Internet to learn how long to cook the pork, the datum is returned as output, and thus is received by the inquirer who in turn perceives it. While reception of the datum is the endpoint of the query process, it is at the same time, as perception, the beginning of a process of taking action. It has become information by being perceived, and now it will serve in its new role as information to affect behavior and several other related outcomes.

Information as a process then, and in particular its sharing across space and time, is the mission of information institutions, and this is a critical point—it is not just the collecting of recorded knowledge that makes an information institution, it is facilitating the efficacy of the process of placing that knowledge into various communicative channels where it can become information. Information institutions share the goal of informing. And all information takes place in the context of culture.

1.3   Alike or Apart?

The natural conclusion of this book's central thesis is that all information institutions—from the Amsterdam's Torture Museum to the *Cumulative Index to Nursing and Allied Health Literature* (CINAHL)—are alike in critical ways. First, they all share the *gravitas* of institutional being. Second, they all share the mission of facilitating an efficacious information process. And, they also all share their diverse cultural positions as socially epistemic actors directed by their cultures in how to disseminate information. These are the synergies that suggest we in the information domain might better consider the following:

- we have a core of scientific theory about information as a process;
- we have a core of scientific theory about the organization of the knowledge that is the data in our information processes;
- despite difference in service missions, we share a core set of prerogatives—collecting, preserving, conserving, circulation; and,
- the professionals who work in these institutions have a common intellectual and theoretical base (i.e., that presented in these bullet points).

Although one has heard various relatively convincing lectures about the history and evolution of information institutions, it is clear that they have evolved as sort of wary neighbors, but not as collective team members. In the virtual world of the 21st century it is time for us to begin to see information institutions as a virtual whole, an interwoven reality. This is made possible in part by the Internet, of course. We can all search Google and get a response quickly, regardless of its accuracy or relevance. On the other hand, it is possible for a scholar (like me, for instance) who is studying instantiation as a phenomenon of bibliographic works, to discover that the phenomenon actually also is present in archives and museum systems as well. That is, there is commonality in work-based function as well as in mission. And the professionals who run these systems have common educational backgrounds as well. It is time to try to understand the virtual reality: information institutions are as much alike as they are different.

1.4   The Promise of Cultural Synergy

By adding to the equation in the preceding sentence one more clause—that information institutions are disseminators of their cultures—we can begin to imagine a rich quilt of interwoven patches. There are dimensions or panels of institutions with similar topical trajectories. There are dimensions or panels of institutions within or near the same cultures. And there are institutions that cross these lines, but have information process-related goals as their mission. These intersecting lines of cultural mission are trajectories for synergy—for allowing us to perceive the universe of information institutions as interconnected and evolving and moving forward in distinct ways for the improvement of the condition of humankind through the building up of its knowledge base and of its information-sharing processes. This is the goal of this book.

References

Furner, Jonathan. 2002. Social epistemology recast as psychological bibliology. *Social Epistemology* 16:5–22.

Furner, Jonathan. 2004. "A brilliant mind": Margaret Egan and social epistemology. *Library Trends* 52 (4): 792–809.

Hjørland, Birger. 1998. Theory and meta-theory of information science: a new interpretation. *Journal of Documentation* 54:606–621.

Shera, Jesse Hauk. 1965. *Libraries and the organization of knowledge*. London: Crosby Lockwood.

Smiraglia, Richard P. 2012. Introduction: theory, knowledge organization, epistemology, culture. In *Cultural frames of knowledge,* eds. P. Richard Smiraglia and Lee Hur-Li, 1–17. Würzburg: Ergon-Verlag.

Chapter 2
The Nature of Information

Abstract To understand the definition of information I look first at the definition of a related term—knowledge, which is that which is known. Recorded knowledge is knowledge that has been recorded in some tangible way. It is a common misperception that what we do in the information field is provide information. Rather, what we do is attempt to comprehend potential human information requirements, and then subsequently collect artifacts from which the correct informational instructions can be extracted, synthesized, and communicated. We provide context, and we filter it through our own expertise. Information is knowledge perceived. In colloquial usage the term "information" is used to refer to documents themselves, or even to simple data. It is crucial to comprehend the fact that information is a dynamic process, which is a crucial aspect of human existence. Finally, information can be culturally cloaked in the subjective experiences of those who experience its process.

I begin this chapter with a simple question: What is information?

A simple enough question on the face of it, no? But, as it turns out, this is a simple question for which there is no simple answer. The term information has no single, simple definition. Rather, the term has been used in different ways by different authors in our field over the course of the last several decades. Be that as it may, I will attempt to bring us to a consensus about the meaning of information for the purpose of the present discussion. I will begin by looking at the definition of a related term—knowledge—and from that I hope to develop an understanding of information that will serve to underpin the remainder of this book.

2.1 Knowledge, Recorded Knowledge, and Information

Knowledge is (simply enough) that which is known. Think about that for a moment. Just what is it that is known? What is it that you think you know? Everything that is in human experience is known. Some things are known to us individually—our sensory memories, for example. We (at least those of us from the USA) know what it smelled like in Grandmother's kitchen on Thanksgiving Day. We know what it felt like to have broken Mother's favorite lamp and have to sit in the corner waiting for Dad to come home. We know how many teabags are left in the cupboard. These

R. P. Smiraglia, *Cultural Synergy in Information Institutions,*
DOI 10.1007/978-1-4939-1249-0_2, © Springer Science+Business Media New York 2014

things are inscribed in our memories and have become a part of who we are and how we function. These things that we know inform our every encounter. And our personal knowledge is cumulative and always growing, moment by moment.

There also is public knowledge—the collective knowledge of humankind in general or of some specific group of people (a community) in particular. This kind of common public knowledge is what we often refer to as culture—it is the context of a social contract. The culture is that set of common knowledge that governs how we relate collectively and individually to each other and to our environment. Denizens of both Canada and the United States experience a holiday known as Thanksgiving, and they all engage in a sort of harvest meal, but the occasions are celebrated at different times and have different cultural contexts. Cultural knowledge is context-dependent. "Thanksgiving" is not necessarily "thanksgiving"—without cultural context the meaning is ambiguous. But, each person who has a perceived recollection of "thanksgiving" has knowledge of thanksgiving.

So we can state unequivocally that knowledge is that which is known. In fact, we can refer to a dictionary definition of knowledge from the *Oxford English Dictionary* online; where we find these major components among the complex of definitions:

(1) Acknowledgement or recognition. (2) The fact or condition of knowing something ....
(3) The faculty of understanding or knowing .... (4) The fact or state of knowing that something is the case....

For the most part (having left out legal and sexual implications) these clauses point to cognition. As a matter of fact, WordNet™'s definition makes that clear: "Cognition, knowledge, noesis (the psychological result of perception and learning and reasoning."

Recorded knowledge is knowledge that has been recorded in some tangible way. Facts are written down and disseminated in books. Musical works are set down on paper so they may be subsequently performed. Performances of musical works are set down in sound recordings so that they may be played and listened to over and over. Landscapes are recreated in paintings, which communicate an aesthetic quality of a view. The same landscape may be recreated in a cartographic document—a map—which communicates the geographical details of a place. All of these are examples of knowledge that has been recorded. The artifacts of recorded knowledge are the tangible records with which we work in the information fields.

It is a common perception—I will state here a *mis*-perception—that what we do in the information field is provide information, as though all we did was to hunt for the right datum to answer a question. "Five," we might say—well, "five what?" a user might ask of us. For without context no datum is useful at all. So what we do is far more complex than the mere provision of facts. We are more complex as a social structure than any search engine (all due respects to Google™ and Yahoo™, or even Freebase™). In fact, what we do is attempt to comprehend potential human information requirements, and then we collect artifacts from which the correct informational instructions can be extracted, synthesized, and communicated. We provide context, and we filter it through our own expertise. It is no error that librarians are among the first sorts of gatekeepers any society generates once it becomes literate.

The books, manuscripts, scores, recordings, paintings, maps, and so forth that are created to record human knowledge are the artifacts that may be collected, organized, and made available for consultation. And these are not just sources of data—they are real extant artifacts. The leather in the bindings was once on a cow, the gilt edge was once on a rock in the ground, the paper was once a tree or some fabric made from a plant; the techniques used to make these artifacts were and are as important as any data recorded in them. So librarians are secondarily the curators of the artifacts of knowledge, and libraries are the great museums of these artifacts of knowledge. Thus the organization of our artifacts, so we might efficiently extract and synthesize their meaning, is critical. Yet it is important to understand that we do not exactly organize knowledge itself—we cannot organize raw knowledge, which has only the form of thoughts in human minds. Rather, we organize the artifacts of knowledge—some authors refer to these as documents. And these documents, or artifacts, subsequently, might be consulted by people who are seeking knowledge.

And that brings us to information. Information is knowledge perceived. That is, what is contained in documents is potential information—it is recorded knowledge that may be consulted for whatever reason. But when that knowledge is consulted and is perceived by the human brain, information is the result. Buckland (1988, p. 30), usefully, has written of this as becoming informed:

> Becoming informed is the term we use to denote the process whereby people's personal knowledge changes in response to the messages they receive. (One could have used the term "information" to denote this process, but it would be ambiguous since the term "information" is more commonly used to denote the data, signals, or messages, i.e., the stuff as well as the process.)

There are several implications of this important concept. First, information is a process and not a thing. Information therefore, is dynamic and not static. Information is what happens to a person when knowledge is perceived, because that new perception alters the person's previously existing knowledge-base. The process of becoming informed can be complex—Cole (1994, p. 475) has suggested a multipart process where concepts enter a "sense data registry" for later use in the modification of a knowledge structure at its highest fundamental level. Information changes people. Which means that information can be very important.

But even Buckland (1988, p. 115) notes the confusion about the term. At least in colloquial usage (and much too often in the library and information press) the term "information" is used to refer to the documents themselves, or to what Buckland has called "the stuff." We must acknowledge this confusion about the most important operative word in our repertoire—for many people, maybe even for most people, information means data and documents. (Even the newest text, Bawden and Robinson (2013), admits to the confusion, using a table to illustrate 11 common differing definitions.) Buckland avoids the terminological confusion by using the term "becoming informed" to denote the process, and leaving the term "information" to its colloquial usage. In this text I will not give in so easily. Acknowledging that there is confusion does not mean we necessarily have to abandon our understanding of information as a dynamic process.

In fact, despite the confusion that arises from colloquial usage and that can be observed in any number of the journals of our field, we can find some affirmation of our assertion that information is process by returning to the dictionary (*Oxford English Dictionary* online):

> 1. The imparting of knowledge in general .... 2a. Knowledge communicated concerning some particular fact, subject or event; that of which one is apprised or told, intelligence, news .... 3a. The action or fact of imparting the knowledge of a fact or occurrence; communication of news; notification....

Interestingly, these definitions all embrace motion or action (once again we are forgoing peculiar associations with sex or the law)—imparting, communication, appraisal, telling, notification—all ways of describing the process of becoming informed. WordNet™ embraces the colloquial multiplicity of meanings but also embraces process:

- a message received and understood;
- knowledge acquired through study or experience or instruction; ...
- a collection of facts from which conclusions may be drawn; and,
- a numerical measure of the uncertainty of an outcome.

Here we see reflected the duality of information as thing—e.g., message, knowledge, facts—but also the processes—received, understood, acquired.

It is crucial, then, to comprehend the fact that information is a dynamic process that has the potential to change people. Information is no static bunch of documents—rather it is a crucial aspect of human existence. Buckland refers to Fairthorne when he asserts that "information is not stuff but a process." Fairthorne (1961) wrote:

> Information is an attribute of the receiver's knowledge and interpretation of the signal, not of the sender's, nor some external omniscient observer's nor of the signal itself.

Fairthorne gives us the other side of our definition that completes its explanation. We see that not only is information the process of becoming informed, but also that information is neither the data nor the vehicle, neither the fact nor the document. Information is a process that happens inside the mind of the one who becomes informed. Information changes a person's knowledge-base, and that in turn affects the way the person relates in community and in the environment. Information changes lives and that makes it a very powerful commodity.

2.2 Scholarship About Information

If you study information in any of its cognate disciplines (like physics, mathematics, social science, communications, journalism, and so on) you will discover a common understanding of information as a pipeline. This is what Day (2000) has called the "conduit metaphor." It comes from an early mathematical theory of communication by Shannon and Weaver that suggested information was like a signal traveling across a wire. If it got to the other end safely it could be received, and if anything went wrong in the process that was called "noise." Noise was thought to be the main problem that prevented the process of information from coming to fruition in any case. Day is a critical theorist, which is a kind of historian—his point is that, not only is this metaphor incomplete, it is misleading, and its power has kept many in the field from exploring more promising approaches.

Imagine approaching your ATM and putting in your card and then you hear a loud noise and *poof* your card is gone. What will you do? The screen offers you no options. Your card is gone. There is no "noise in the channel" here, instead the system has crashed and taken you with it. This I think is Day's point—we need to get past the blinders of this metaphor so we can truly understand the power of information as an existential phenomenon. When I tell you to read Buckland, I have informed you. When I step on a tack the pain has informed by body of an intrusion. When you water your hibiscus and it stands up straight you have informed the plant of its nutrition. And on and on I could go.

In fact, Michel Menou (1995, p. 482) wrote a series of articles about a potential theory of information. His most important contribution (arguably) was his insistence on three elements: semantics, syntax, and paradigm. In other words, context is critical for the comprehension of information—senders and receivers alike (to refer to the conduit metaphor) need meaning (semantics), rules (syntax), and context (paradigm) to make "sense" of information tasks. Menou, therefore, called us to attend to the problem of sense-making as information professionals.

One attempt at a comprehensive review of information was by Bates (2006). She attempted to draw together several theories of information from different disciplines, including physics and biology. She came to the conclusion that information could be described as (p. 1044): "the pattern of organization of matter and energy." She then draws on disparate theories to suggest (not unlike Buckland) that there are different kinds of information—some naturally encoded, some genetically embedded, and some external to the body. Of course, her point of view is controversial. Barely a year later in the same journal Birger Hjørland, a very important Danish philosopher of information science and knowledge organization, took issue with nearly all of Bates' points. Hjørland (2007) said that we have to consider whether information is situational or objective. Although his text was more complex than this, he essentially suggested that information is situational, emergent, and evolutionary—in other words, vague until interpreted. Notice that his point of view accords nicely with Menou's notion of sense-making and with Buckland's notion of the process of information. This is a semiotic point of view—semiotics is the science of signs, meaning that all perception is constantly interpretatively mutable—but it has some appeal as an explanation of the difficulties we have as professionals whose job it is to provide information. And it speaks exactly to why we have to be attentive to more than just finding data as answers to questions, because information needs are constantly evolving.

In a fascinating study conducted in 2004–2005 an Israeli information scientist named Chaim Zins conducted a Delphi study of information scientists worldwide to see whether he could generate a common definition of "information." Delphi method is often used to consult a set of scholars about generating a research agenda for the future. This time it revealed all of the disparity in the discipline—the 57 scholars came up with 57 different definitions, and refused to budge or to agree even a little bit with each others' points of view. The 57 scholars drew 28 different maps of the discipline. In the end all that could be generated as consensus from the study was a list of essential components: data, information, knowledge (Zins 2007). These, he asserts, are the fundamental building blocks of the discipline. The problem is, as Zins admits (p. 479) the field supports diversified meanings for all three.

Which brings us back to Hjørland who with Capurro (2003) acknowledged that there are two main schools of thought, information as an object (a thing) and as a sign (a subjective concept). But they also concluded (interestingly enough, 3 years before Hjorland's public dispute with Bates) that interdisciplinary understanding is important. In fact, in the next chapter we will see how Bates (among others) has called for an interdisciplinary comprehension of concepts of information, and how we alone in the field of information are well prepared to deal with this interdisciplinary schizophrenia.

More recently the concept of information has been the subject of books in the general marketplace. An early and concise example is Floridi (2010), which is a survey of the meaning of information within and across several disciplines—mathematics, semantics, physics, biology, and economics—together with an ethical summary. Floridi places his text within the context of information revolution and information society—in essence a social context—and suggests a common life-cycle of information that includes a sequence of phases (p. 4): occurrence, transmission, processing and management, and usage. Interestingly this sequence moves across the boundaries we've already encountered. That is, here information moves from sign to object, from sense-making process to thing. At the time of publication of this book Floridi holds a chair in the philosophy of information at the University of Hertfordshire—a philosopher and author about ethics and thus a scholar able to take a broad overview of information. A thesis of his book is that human society is experiencing a revolution in which a reassessment of humanity's role in the universe is shifting from a perception of material reality to one of information. He characterizes this with everyday examples—a shift, say, from material assets to virtual assets, as from holding a room full of LP music recordings to having, instead, digital access to musical sound. The difference is profound and has profound consequences as society shifts from object to process—the reverse of the sequence he suggests—in its comprehension of information. In 2011 James Gleick, a historian, produced the very impressive (and very long) history of information, moving deftly from a story of talking drums to a conclusion that society might face information exhaustion. Gleick does not so much define information as trace a history of the idea of information as a cultural and social phenomenon. His account of the story of Claude Shannon and the evolution of the conduit theory of information is fascinating reading, and it helps us understand perhaps the role of that theory in our own information field. In Gleick's text, what he calls "the information" is not a scientific phenomenon (although some of its iterations are so presented) so much as a social one, neither process nor thing, then, but rather a large part of human experience.

Finally (at least for now), Mai (2013) reviews much of the material reviewed here and more (and in more detail) as an approach to discussing the concept of information quality. Like those cited above, he settles on two kinds of information, one kind that is quantifiably measurable and another kind that is psychological (p. 676). He concludes that the most useful approach is to perceive information as a kind of sign (p. 686) "to facilitate the exchange and production of meaning," process and thing intertwined. Bawden and Robinson (2014) survey the concept and usage of information in five domains, arriving at the description of what they call a "binary divide" (p. 131) between objective and subjective, comparable to (or perhaps parallel with) Mai's notion that information can be measurable or psychological. And Furner (2014) reviews the multiple ontological commitments of information theorists, all outside of our information field, suggesting in the end that it is useful and appropriate, because of our own ontological pluralism, that we should have no single definition.

2.3 Many Ways of Information

The word "information" is used in many ways both colloquially and in the information discipline. In this chapter I have asserted that information is knowledge perceived. Knowledge—things that are known, both communally (as in the knowledge base that defines a culture) and individually—can be recorded in some tangible way. The records of knowledge can be organized to provide access both to the records themselves (as in a library) and to the knowledge they contain (as in information retrieval systems). Information is the process of becoming informed—neither the data nor the vehicle, neither the fact nor the document.

And as we have seen from this review, information can be culturally cloaked in the subjective experiences of those who experience its process. It is this cloak of cultural context that gives information its synergistic promise.

References

Bates, Marcia J. 2006. Fundamental forms of information. *Journal of the American Society for Information Science and Technology* 57:1033–1045.

Bawden, David, and Lyn Robinson. 2013. *Introduction to information science.* Chicago: Neal-Schuman.

Bawden, David, and Lyn Robinson. 2014. Mind the gap: Transitions between concepts of information in varied domains. In *Theories of information, communication and knowledge: A multidisciplinary approach. Studies in history and philosophy of science,* eds. Fidelia Ibekwe-SanJuan and Thomas M. Dousa., 121–141. 344 vols. Dordrecht: Springer.

Buckland, Michael K. 1988. *Library services in theory and context.* 2nd ed. Oxford: Pergamon Press.

Capurro, Rafael and Birger Hjørland. 2003. The concept of information. *Annual Review of Information Science and Technology* 37:343–411.

Cole, Charles. 1994. Operationalizing the notion of information as a subjective construct. *Journal of the American Society for Information Science* 45:475.

Day, Ronald. 2000. The 'conduit metaphor' and the nature and politics of information studies. *Journal of the American Society for Information Science* 51:805–811.

Fairthorne, R. A. 1961. *Towards information retrieval*. London: Butterworths.

Floridi, Luciano. 2010. *Information: A very short introduction*. Oxford: Oxford University Press.

Furner, Jonathan. 2014. Information without information studies. In *Theories of information, communication and knowledge: A multidisciplinary approach. Studies in history and philosophy of science,* eds. Fidelia Ibekwe-SanJuan and Thomas M. Dousa, 143–179. 344 vols. Dordrecht: Springer.

Gleick, James. 2011. *The information: A history, a theory, a flood*. New York: Pantheon Books.

Hjørland, Birger. 2007. Information—objective or subjective/situational? *Journal of the American Society for Information Science and Technology* 58:1448–1456.

Mai, Jens-Erik. 2013. The quality and qualities of information. *Journal of the American Society for Information Science and Technology* 64:675–688.

Menou, Michel J. 1995. The impact of information—II. concepts of information and its value. *Information Processing and Management* 31:479–490.

Zins, Chaim. 2007. Conceptual approaches for defining data, information, and knowledge. *Journal of the American Society for Information Science and Technology* 58:479–493.

Chapter 3
What is (are) Information Studies?

Abstract What are library and information science, information science, and information studies? Science involves rigorously articulated methodological activity that leads to the observation of phenomena. For most of the twentieth century library and information studies took place in the context of fields known variously as library science, information science, later as library and information science, then as information studies, and only recently as simply information itself. But this sequence of names reveals an evolution as well. In the first decades of the twentieth century, a new movement began to dub certain grant-endowed and technologically focused schools as "iSchools." The field of information (or information studies) commonly is acknowledged to consist of several interlocking sub-disciplines, each of which has developed its own tools and principles, and in some of which theory is beginning to emerge. "Information," of "Information Studies," is an emerging discipline that has evolved from the convergence of librarianship and information as a science with other components of cognitive science. Rigorous scientific research has begun to yield a small base of theoretical knowledge as well, particularly into the essential properties of information (the process) and its carriers (knowledge artifacts and systems that organize and provide access to them). The discipline is itself a synergistic force because the object of our research is knowledge itself, and its potential as information; the role of the field is to isolate and define a shared base of principles that inform the information professions.

Now that we know (or think we know) what information is, we move on to another set of questions. What constitutes information studies? What is information science? What does information science have to do with libraries? For that matter, what is library science? Why do we so often see the formulation "library-and-information science?" What about all of the other kinds of information institutions?

3.1 Science

Perhaps we should begin with a simpler question: what is science? Science can be thought of as any consciously premeditated form of inquiry. Our dictionary gives the following enlightenment (*Oxford English Dictionary* online):

R. P. Smiraglia, *Cultural Synergy in Information Institutions,*   17
DOI 10.1007/978-1-4939-1249-0_3, © Springer Science+Business Media New York 2014

1a. The state or fact of knowing; knowledge or cognizance *of* something specified or implied; also, with wider reference, knowledge (more or less extensive) as a personal attribute …. 2a. Knowledge acquired by study; acquaintance with or mastery of any department of learning …. 3a. A particular branch of knowledge or study; a recognized department of learning …. 4a. In a more restricted sense: A branch of study which is concerned either with a connected body of demonstrated truths or with observed facts systematically classified and more or less colligated by being brought under general laws, and which includes trustworthy methods for the discovery of new truth within its own domain.

According to this definition we can see that science involves rigorously articulated methodological activity that leads to the observation of phenomena. Science also involves the subsequent use of such methodologically derived observations for the description and explanation of phenomena, which in turn can lead to their theoretical explanation. Colloquially the term science often is reserved for the description of natural phenomena. But in the broader realm of academe, many activities fall under the definition of scientific inquiry. In fact, in the academy the sciences are distinguished as a form of study only from the humanities and the arts. So at one end of a spectrum we can say that science is methodological activity that is neither humanistic in origin nor artistic in purpose.

3.2   Library Science, Information Science, and Library-and-Information-Science

Our discipline, which in a few paragraphs I will begin to refer to simply as information (and which, heretofore, I have called "the information field"), comprises many individual sub-disciplines, all of which have in common the pursuit of knowledge about the process of becoming informed. For most of the twentieth century these studies took place in the context of fields known variously as library science, information science, later as library and information science, then as information studies, and only recently as simply information itself. I will examine the historical development of the field in a subsequent chapter (see Chap. 4). But for now let us attempt to understand these terms in the context of a brief historical outline so that we may see how they have preceded the term information. It remains critical throughout this examination to remember that the purpose of the discipline is the pursuit of knowledge about information—the process of becoming informed.

Library science is a term that grew out of the field of librarianship after schools for librarians became associated with leading universities. Formal education for librarianship began in the United States with Melville Dewey's School of Library Economy, which was first held at (but was not a part of) Columbia University in 1876. By the late 1920s the field had grown sufficiently that schools had begun to be established in major universities. In the late 1920s there was a major attempt to establish intellectual rigor in the field so as to begin to develop an underlying theoretical paradigm for librarianship and its emerging sub-disciplines. It was from this effort that the term library science was born at the Graduate Library School at the University of Chicago. Pierce Butler, then a professor at Chicago, wrote a text titled *Introduction to Library Science* in which he outlined the parameters of science and ways in which they could be applied to the investigation of questions that concern librarians. His concluding phrases suggest the central problem he faced in creating from librarianship the academic discipline of library science (Butler 1933, p. 113, 115):

> Still another possible benefit... is that of creating for librarianship a sense of professional unity.... Certainly none of these things will be possible until librarianship turns its attention from process to function. When it does this it will perceive its phenomena in terms of a library science.

Simultaneously, the field known as documentation was developing alongside librarianship. Documentalists, primarily in Europe, were concerned with solving the problem of the dispersal of primary source materials and particularly with the rapid dissemination of scientific results. It was from documentalists that the mechanization of tools for retrieving data—bibliographic and otherwise—grew into the field now known as information science. In 1961 The American Documentation Institute changed its name to The American Society for Information Science (in 2012 the name changed to The Association for Information Science and Technology). Information scientists now work primarily in the arena of systems for and theory underlying information storage and retrieval.

W. Boyd Rayward argued in 1983 that librarianship had converged toward information science. He wrote (p. 354):

> I attribute a disciplinary convergence, insofar as it has occurred, to essentially two factors. The first was the thoughtful recognition by leaders in the fields of library science and information science that they were committed to finding solutions to the same general problems, despite differences in terminology and orientation. The second was the increasing importance of the computer.

Throughout the 1980s evidence of the convergence Rayward suggested became clearer as more authors used the conjoined term library-and-information-science, and as increasing numbers of graduate schools preparing librarians took the conjoined term into their official names. In 1968 Harold Borko offered a definition of the entire discipline (p. 3):

> That discipline that investigates the properties and behavior of infomation, the forces governing the flow in information, and the means of processing information for optimum accessability.

Here we see the convergence that Rayward has described. The discipline Borko defines is one that is concerned with the nature of the phenomenon of information (information science), the forces and means that govern the flow of information (institutions and professions such as libraries, archives, and information centers, and forces such as information policy), and systems for accessibility (everything from information storage and retrieval databases to library circulation systems).

3.3 Information Studies

However, information has never been solely the province of graduate schools that educated librarians. In Machlup and Mansfield's 1983 volume *The Study of Information: Interdisciplinary Messages*, an entire prologue was devoted to the concept of "Cultural Diversity in Studies of Information." In this essay we are introduced to a lengthy list of disciplines that all treat information in some way. These include: cybernetics, semiotics and linguistics, computer science, artificial intelligence, robotics, system theory, the meta-discipline referred to as "cognitive science," and even the very narrowly defined "information theory" derived from Shannon's mathematical theory of communication. At the conclusion of Chap. 2 we saw, once again, how the search for a unified definition of information keeps returning to the clusters of domains (or disciplines) that do have precise commitments to the meaning of information. One might reasonably marvel at the ubiquitousness of possession of meanings of information.

Be that as it may, in the 1990s graduate schools began to broaden their course offerings to include more and more of these disciplines. In particular, schools such as those at Rutgers University and Drexel University merged programs in communications, archives, library and information science, and information transfer to create schools of "information studies." Such schools typically continued to offer terminal masters degrees for librarians and archivists. But they also included undergraduate programs in information transfer that were designed to educate people for the rapidly expanding information industries, including software development, online research and data provision, and all aspects of Internet technology. The complex of degrees at these schools also has expanded to include interdisciplinary doctoral degrees in information studies that do not require preparation in librarianship for admission, and in which students are required to work not only in the broadly defined areas of information studies, but in external disciplines as well. In the first decade of the twentieth century, a new movement began to dub certain grant-endowed and technologically focused schools as "iSchools" (for schools of information, but incorporating the now-iconic "i"-usage from the computer industry). The iSchool at the University of Toronto was among the first to incorporate graduate programs in museology into its information stream.

Of 58 programs accredited by the American Library Association under the rubric "library and information studies," the majority (24) are called programs of "library and information science," and another 17 are called programs of "library and information studies" or just "information studies." (The remainder employ a bewildering array of terms, all but one of which include the word "information.") Five brave institutions have some formulation of "School of Information," thus asserting the possibility of a definable theoretical base for all of the aforementioned sub-disciplines and the professions that rely on them.

Another trend has been the development of bachelor's degree programs in "information studies" beginning with the University of Pittsburgh in 1979. These programs are designed to meet the need for college-educated workers for the information industry. Increasingly, doctoral programs aligned with these schools are called programs of "information studies," and many do not require a master's degree in "library and information" for admission.

3.4   And What of Science?

Despite the name of the various schools, we must not lose sight of the fact that information studies—or, if you will, information—still involves the heavy integration of technology, professional practice, and theory. And theory must be the result of rigorous scientific inquiry. But it is important for us to keep in mind that ours is a very young discipline. Formal schools of librarianship date only from the 1870s—barely more than a century ago. Scientific rigor applied to the problems of librarianship dates only from the late 1920s—still less than a century ago. In that time, scholars have made remarkable progress at cumulating research and at tentative suggestions of theoretical bases. Other, older disciplines can call on hundreds of years of observation, research, and writing that inform the technologies that rely on them. Forensic anthropology for instance—the discipline that allows criminologists to discover the means and circumstances of life and death from the tiniest remnants of a human body—relies on centuries of knowledge of the human anatomy and its reaction to literally thousands of phenomena.

In information studies we have a small amount of theory, derived from research. We have a much larger body of principles derived from common experience, which both underlie professional practice and provide hypotheses for research. In time, when sufficient research has accumulated, some of these principles will evolve into a larger body of theory. That is the importance of continued rigorous analysis, particularly into the essential properties of information (the process) and its carriers (knowledge artifacts and systems that organize and provide access to them). It is also vitally important that archival and museum studies, which now are underrepresented in schools of information studies, should be part of the mainstream of thought and research. Institutional synergy will require that.

3.5   The Components of Information Studies

The field of information studies commonly is acknowledged to consist of several interlocking sub-disciplines, each of which has developed its own tools and principles, and in some of which theory is beginning to emerge. In this book I will consider the following sub-disciplines to comprise information studies:

- Knowledge organization, including traditional bibliography and bibliographic control;
- Information as entity, including information service;

- Information retrieval, including systems for rapid access to specific data;
- Information transfer, including the burgeoning commercial information industry and the Internet;
- Communications, behavioral psychology, and the cultural role of information;
- System design, and human-computer interaction; and,
- Information policy and intellectual freedom.

3.6   Into a Discipline of Information

"Information," of "Information Studies," is an emerging discipline that has evolved from the convergence of librarianship and information as a science with other components of cognitive science. Rigorous scientific research has begun to yield a small base of theoretical knowledge as well, particularly into the essential properties of information (the process) and its carriers (knowledge artifacts and systems that organize and provide access to them). A famous paper by Bates (1999) explored the idea of our discipline as "substrate" (a geographical phenomenon, although "subfloor" might also be a useful analogy), making the point that the domain is much more than the sum of its explicit parts because the subjects of its analysis are all of the other knowledge disciplines. That is, our discipline is itself a synergistic force because the object of our research is knowledge itself, and its potential as information. I will continue to explore this idea in subsequent chapters. The responsibility of information institutions is itself a kind of synergy. Therefore there must also be a shared base of principles that inform the information professions. This is the subject of the next chapter.

References

Bates, Marcia J. 1999. The invisible substrate of information science. *Journal of the American Society for Information Science* 50:1043–1050.

Borko, H. 1968. Information science: What is it? *American Documentation* 19:3–5.

Butler, Pierce. 1933. *An introduction to library science.* Chicago: University of Chicago Press.

Machlup, Fritz, and Una Mansfield. eds. 1983. *The study of information: Interdisciplinary messages.* New York: Wiley.

Rayward, W. Boyd. 1983. Library and information sciences: disciplinary differentiation, competition, and convergence. In *The study of information: Interdisciplinary messages*, eds. Fritz Machlup and Una Mansfield, 343–405. New York: Wiley.

Chapter 4
The Synergistic Information Professions: Applications of the Information Process

Abstract Information studies is the set of basic principles that underlie the information professions. Information professions are those in which the theories and principles are those of the information process—in other words, those professions that provide services that allow people to become informed. For purposes of this overview the information professions are grouped into two main categories—institutions (libraries, archives, museums) and organizations (knowledge management, management information systems, information architecture). Librarianship is the profession that has evolved around the management of libraries—institutions that house deliberately-constructed collections of publications for the common use of a group of people. Archives and Records Management are professions that manage the raw data of history, the sources from which scholars create filtered narratives; their role is to preserve the historical record of society. Information professionals who work in museums might be, or might work alongside, archeologists, anthropologists, classicists, and scientists for whom the acquisition and analysis of artifacts is a primary science. Museums have archivists whose job is to focus on the internal records of the museum. There will also be conservationists and preservationists whose job it is to see that the artifacts are maintained and not allowed to deteriorate. Knowledge management is the largely corporate school of thought having to do with the means by which organizations create and govern their collective knowledge base. The information process is central to the roles of all information professionals, facilitating the transfer of messages among humans for the purpose of allowing them to become informed. Information professionals all serve as gatekeepers in their cultures.

We can think of information as an emerging discipline that has evolved from the convergence of librarianship and information science with other components of cognitive science. Scientific effort has been directed toward answering questions about the essential properties of information (the process) and its carriers (knowledge artifacts and systems that organize and provide access to them). But in a very fundamental sense, information studies is the set of basic principles that underlie the information professions.

A profession is a group of people who employ common skills to accomplish some end, usually a service. Professions are usually the product, or application, of a set of common theories and principles. Professionals often are distinguished by

R. P. Smiraglia, *Cultural Synergy in Information Institutions,*
DOI 10.1007/978-1-4939-1249-0_4, © Springer Science+Business Media New York 2014

membership in a professional association or society, which upholds the application of these principles, generates research into new theories, disseminates new applications, and provides a common set of ethics to govern professional activity. Law, medicine, dentistry, education, nursing—these are a few examples of professions that are prominent in our society.

Information professions are those in which the theories and principles are those of the information process—in other words, those professions that provide services that allow people to become informed. Like other professions, the information professions are populated with highly-skilled professionals, many of whom hold accredited degrees from graduate institutions. Others may hold academic rather than professional credentials—many archivists hold masters degrees from departments of history, management-information-systems professionals hold degrees from schools of business, etc. And increasingly, dual-masters degree programs are being inaugurated to allow professionals to get both professional and academic credentials at the same time. The information professions are also shepherded and maintained by a group of professional societies such as the American Library Association or the Society of American Archivists, for example, which exist to set best practice, to generate applied research and disseminate results, to promulgate new applications, and to maintain ethical standards.

Professionals are distinguished in our society from other types of workers by their practice of their craft. Professionals tend to work in institutions but in highly autonomous positions that allow them to exercise their judgment as situations arise. A professional is more likely to be career-oriented than job-oriented. This is a critical distinction, because a self-generated career will require a professional to keep constantly abreast of new theoretical and technological developments. Also, career paths will lead persons from institution to institution, rather than up a career-ladder (as is found in the corporate environment). Most information professionals work in not-for-profit settings, and most work in large institutions. Increasingly information professionals are found in free-lance work environments or in commercial institutions that provide specific information services. And, increasing proportions of the very mobile urban population are information professionals. In this chapter I will survey the information professions and the institutions or settings in which they are practiced.

4.1   The Professions: An Overview

For purposes of this overview the information professions will be grouped into two main categories, in each of which can be seen a commonality of application of the information process to quite specific problem sets. These two main categories are institutions (libraries, archives, museums) and organizations (knowledge management, management information systems, information architecture). This grouping can be seen as a continuum for the practice of the information process. It is an imperfect continuum because the categories are not entirely mutually exclusive. That is, there are corporate librarians who work in for- profit organizations, and there are academic knowledge management specialists. However, one could argue that librarianship is the oldest of the information professions (dating to ancient times) and knowledge management among the newest (having arisen near the end of the twentieth-century). Consequently, this arrangement will allow us to see the evolution of applications of the information process, which after all is the commonality shared across the professions.

4.2 Institutions

4.2.1 Librarianship

Librarianship is the profession that has evolved around the management of libraries—institutions that house deliberately-constructed collections of publications for the common use of a group of people. The purpose of librarianship is always to supply the needs of the institution's clientele or patrons. Often this means helping people to determine the relevant facts—that is, the truth—from among the vast store of recorded knowledge. Libraries and librarianship have two unifying features: the cultural role of the institution, and the social role of the profession.

Libraries are institutions generated and supported by the societies in which they exist for the purpose of preserving and disseminating the collective knowledge of those societies' cultures. Jesse Shera wrote that the traditional role of the library is the preservation and transmission of the cultural heritage. He continued (Shera 1976, p. 49):

> If [the library] departs too far from the attitudes and value system of its own culture, it is certain to be in trouble. The library, then, reflects a particular "world view," a "paradigm" to use Thomas Kuhn's term, or an "image," to borrow from Kenneth Boulding. Such paradigms, or images, may change through time in response to changes in the culture, and the library that is unable to adjust to such alterations may discover that it no longer has a social purpose and the culture has cut it adrift.

Shera has reference here to Kenneth Boulding's *The Image: Knowledge in Life and Society* (Boulding 1956) and to Thomas Kuhn's *The Structure of Scientific Revolutions* (Kuhn 1996). All libraries have an important cultural role to play. University libraries not only support teaching and research, but they preserve and disseminate the academic culture of the specific university in which they are found. Public libraries are much more than repositories of children's books, mysteries, city directories and cookbooks. Public libraries preserve and disseminate the culture of the communities in which they are found. And so on and so on, through the list of types of libraries. The colloquial image of the library as a warehouse for books is very wrong. Michael Gorman and Walt Crawford celebrated the diversity of libraries. They wrote (1995, p. 118):

> Libraries are places to learn—places in which to become knowledgeable. They also provide
> entertainment, serendipity, the opportunity to find out about a host of practical matters, and
> all the treasures of the human mind... Libraries are social places—centers of their com-
> munities, campuses, and institutions.

Librarianship then—the profession that encompasses the creation, management and preservation of libraries as institutions—is especially denoted by its social role as the profession that collects, preserves and disseminates recorded knowledge.

Librarians (and their libraries) play pivotal roles in the cultures that generate them. James O'Donnell has suggested that librarians have been critical historically in the dissemination of knowledge, functioning as "acolytes" to the scholars of the early centuries of the common era. But in the knowledge market of the late twentieth century, O'Donnell suggests that librarians may assume a more primary role, especially in the university. He writes (1998, p. 90, emphasis original):

> The thing that I *will* be willing to pay for as oceans of data lap at my door is help in finding
> and filtering that flood to suit my needs. Among participants in the production, dissemina-
> tion, and consumption of knowledge today, librarians have already made that kind of skill
> their specialty. They have, moreover, already led the way into the new information environ-
> ment, for academics at least. They are caught between the rising demand for information
> from their customers (faculty and students) and rising supply of that information and prices
> for it from their suppliers, and so have already been making pragmatic decisions about the
> importance of ownership versus access, print versus electronic, and so on. Can we imagine
> a time in our universities when librarians are the well-paid principals and teachers their
> mere acolytes? I do not think we can or should rule out that possibility.

The unifying element in librarianship—the profession—is the search for what Jesse Shera called "truth." That is, because libraries exist to preserve and disseminate a culture, they must by definition consist of carefully selected materials, which are presided over and disseminated by well-educated professionals who lend the weight of their professional decision about relevance and truth to the information transaction that takes place when library users encounter collected materials. Jesse Shera wrote that the unity that defined librarianship over and against other professions was the search for truth (1976, pp. 52–53):

> The librarian... must relentlessly search for Truth fragmented "into a thousand pieces"
> by that "great blooming buzzing confusion" that is human experience. What motivates
> the good librarian is not, as has been so frequently said, the love of books, but love of
> Truth—Truth, wherever and in whatever form it may be found. For the end of knowledge is
> wisdom, and wisdom is the power to perceive truth in all its relationships—therein lies the
> unity of librarianship in all its forms and practices, and for all its patrons, however diverse
> they may be.

The works that are selected for acquisition are those that have been determined by a publisher to be worthy of being recorded in print, and that have subsequently been selected by a librarian who has determined them worthy of preservation and dissemination in the community that is directly being served. This means that every work in a library has been twice-chosen: once by a publisher, whose editors and perhaps peers of the author have all determined the work to be worthy of dissemination; and then a second time by a librarian who has determined that the work should be preserved and made available to library users who seek the truth. The search for the truth that Shera writes about is in fact the unity that identifies all aspects of librarianship.

Librarianship may take many manifestations from the lone individual who selects, acquires, catalogs, interprets, and manages a single collection to the highly specialized practice of bibliography or cataloging in disciplinary-based departments found in some of the world's immense research libraries. Michael Buckland (1988, p. 17) noted the ambiguous use of the term librarianship to denote both "a set of techniques" and "the occupation of those who are known as librarians." These techniques and occupations are many and varied. One way to look at them is to consider the functions performed by librarians that cut across institutional settings—all of which are related to the central problem of the search for the truth. Another way is to examine the institutional contexts in which libraries are found—all of which demonstrate the cultural role of libraries.

Librarianship can be defined by the functions librarians perform. These are:

1. Collection development (selection, acquisition, and maintenance of works);
2. Bibliographic control (cataloging, classification, and arrangement of materials);
3. Information service (reference assistance); and,
4. Access to materials (circulation and interlibrary loan).

Collection development librarians decide what works have sufficient worth to become part of a library's collection. That is, after publishers, collection development librarians have the most important social role in determining which works will be preserved and disseminated over time. A decision to acquire a work means that a determination has been made at some level that the given work has value to the institution's clientele and therefore to its culture. Once the province of selection and acquisition alone, in recent times collection development has come to incorporate the functions of preservation and conservation. That is, collection development librarians not only decide which works to acquire for the collection, but they also play a decisive role in determining which works will be preserved into the future (for works that will be preserved through reprography (i.e., reproduction)), and also which specific artifacts must be conserved (made physically stable so as to last physically into the future).

Librarians who work in bibliographic control are those who catalog, classify and arrange the works for retrieval. Cataloging is the production of a tool for the retrieval of specific bibliographic entities held by a library. Cataloging involves the creation of a bibliographic record that stands in the retrieval tool as a surrogate for the bibliographic entity itself. Classification involves the assignment of works to categories so that they may be retrieved in the context of works to which they relate. In most North American libraries classification is also used for shelf arrangement of materials, so as to facilitate browsing and serendipitous retrieval of works by library users. Librarians who fulfill these functions serve the first level of interpretation in a library collection, as they determine what subjects the works treat and with which points of view. These interpretations, objectively applied, subtly influence the usability of library materials.

Information service librarians work in the traditional realms of reference and interlibrary loan, and also often facilitate bibliographic instruction. Information service librarians stand on the last line of decision-making about the truth of data in library collections as they bring to bear their knowledge of the whole of the bibliographical universe as well as of the specific library collection in which they function on each specific request for data. Information service librarians must be schooled in the depth and breadth of their collections, and they must also be able to swiftly navigate the shoals of the bibliographic retrieval systems devised by the bibliographic control apparatus. Like librarians who work in bibliographic control, information service librarians serve to interpret the collection to the library's users.

The fourth generic function of librarianship is direct access to materials. Librarians who work in access services are responsible for the management of the physical well-being of a library's artifacts, which may range from books to sound recordings to video games to websites. Circulation librarians also are responsible for the management of the access services, and in particular for the circulation function itself. Because this requires the library to have a record of who has which items at any given moment, circulation librarians have occasionally become the targets of law enforcement agencies seeking to discover what, exactly, a given criminal suspect might have borrowed. Such a clear violation of the freedom of privacy and the freedom of speech cannot be tolerated in a free society, and circulation librarians can, and often do, find themselves on the front lines of the Bill of Rights, as responsible for protecting users' privacy as for protecting the library's artifacts.

Librarianship can also be defined according to the institutional contexts in which libraries are found. These are:

1. Public
2. School
3. Academic
4. Research
5. Corporate
6. Special
7. Subject-based (math, classics, modern languages, history, LIS, etc.)
8. Profession-based (art, music, medicine, law, business, etc.)

Each of these types of libraries exists to serve a primary constituency, and thereby serve to preserve and disseminate the culture that has generated the library. Public libraries are usually tax-supported educational institutions that play pivotal roles in the information process and the political and cultural life of their communities. School libraries serve much the same function, usually in the public school districts of a community, providing educational resources to teachers and pupils alike. In public and school libraries the collections will tend to change with some rapidity as the cultural milieu itself evolves over time. Public and school libraries are regularly weeded—that is old and under-used materials are discarded to make way for newer and more useful materials. Public and school libraries may also be governed in part by citizen boards, which oversee the librarians in issues such as budget priorities, collection-development and circulation policies, etc.

Academic and research libraries may be tax-supported when they exist in public-supported institutions, such as state or city colleges or universities. Or, when they exist to serve private institutions, such as private colleges, universities, and institutes, they may be supported largely by endowments and private monies. Either way, academic and research libraries usually exist to collect and preserve the totality of recorded knowledge in the fields they serve. Because it cannot ever be determined which materials might be of importance in the distant future, academic and especially research libraries strive for exhaustivity in their collections. A high priority then, is the preservation and conservation of resources that are physically deteriorating. Also, because of the economic burden of collecting exhaustively in any field, another high priority for academic and research libraries is inter-institutional cooperation, by which neighboring institutions pledge to collect exhaustively in one subject area in return for a pledge of unrestricted access for its scholars in other institution's collections.

Corporate and special libraries are those that serve specific corporations or industries, and their librarians are responsible for providing information management to support the goals of the organization or corporation. Special libraries are often found in corporations and private businesses, but also in government agencies, museums, and hospitals. And special librarians may be employed in free-lance situations or by consulting firms. Consequently, special librarians may or may not have collection-development responsibilities, but they are more likely than academic or public librarians to have responsibility for knowledge-management activities, such as providing summary reports of existing data to support a specific problem-resolution situation.

Subject- and profession-based libraries also exist, although rarely independently. That is, most subject- or profession-based libraries are themselves units of larger academic or public libraries. A notable exception is medical libraries, which are usually units of medical schools, and usually not therefore component parts of general libraries in the universities that host them. Subject-based libraries are often divisions of university or research libraries and include fields such as mathematics, classics, modern languages, history and philosophy, library and information studies, geography, physics, engineering, chemistry, etc.—essentially any distinct teaching or research discipline within a university. Similarly, profession-based libraries serve professional schools such as art, music, medicine, law, business, etc. Sometimes both functions are fulfilled in a single unit, as for example a music library in a university or conservatory of music, which is likely to support musicological research, and music education in addition to performance study.

I noted earlier that professionals often are distinguished by membership in a professional association or society. Such organizations generate standards for professional performance, serve as catalysts for research into expanded applications of the theoretical base, and often provide a common set of ethics. Also, professional societies provide a community for professionals from diverse geographical locations who meet together periodically to discuss their common problems and to share their wisdom about specific applications.

Librarianship is supported by a network of professional organizations, beginning with the American Library Association (ALA). The ALA serves as a national professional society for librarians of all types working in all sorts of institutions. ALA also incorporates divisions and round tables that serve to allow greater community for specialist librarians. The divisions are:

AASL—American Association of School Librarians
ALCTS—Association for Library Collections & Technical Services
ALSC—Association for Library Service to Children
ACRL—Association of College and Research Libraries
ASCLA—Association of Specialized and Cooperative Library Agencies
LITA—Library & Information Technology Association
LLAMA—Library Leadership & Management Association
PLA—Public Library Association
RUSA—Reference and User Services Association
United for Libraries
YALSA—Young Adult Library Services Association.

Notice that almost all of ALA's divisions bear names that include the word "association"—that is, ALA's divisions constitute distinct professional associations themselves, in addition to the role they play as divisions of the American Library Association. Each division publishes newsletters and journals, and many also supervise the publication of monographic works as well.

ALA also comprises several round tables. Round tables, like interest groups, are more casually organized membership units that exist to promote "a field of librarianship not within the scope of any single division." ALA round tables are:

EMIERT—Ethnic & Multicultural Information Exchange
Exhibits Round Table (ERT)
Federal and Armed Forces Libraries Round Table (FAFLRT)
Games & Gaming Round Table—(GameRT)
Gay, Lesbian, Bisexual, Transgendered Round Table (GLBTRT)
Government Documents Round Table (GODORT)
Intellectual Freedom Round Table (IFRT)
International Relations Round Table (IRRT)
Learning RT (LearnRT)
Library History (LHRT)
Library Instruction Round Table
Library Research (LRRT)
Library Support Staff Interests Round Table (LSSIRT)
Map and Geospatial Information (MAGERT)
New Members Round Table (NMRT)
Retired Members Round Table (RMRT)
Round Table Coordinating Assembly
Social Responsibilities Round Table (SRRT)
Staff Organizations (SORT)
Video Round Table (VRT)

In addition to the ALA, there are state and regional library associations in every part of the United States (e.g., the California Library Association, or the New England Library Association). Also, there are many very strong national professional associations for librarians in other countries—two to which ALA is most closely tied are The Library Association (of the United Kingdom) and the Canadian Library Association. For specialist librarians there are several prominent associations of specialist librarians (e.g., the Medical Library Association, the Law Library Association, the Art Libraries Society of North America, the Music Library Association, and the Special Library Association). At the international level, most associations of librarians and information professionals are represented in the International Federation of Library Associations and Institutions (IFLA).

4.2.2 Archives and Records Management

Archives and Records Management are professions that parallel librarianship in many ways, but are distinctly different in the social role their practitioners play. Archives are the repositories of primary sources. That is, unlike libraries, which house works that are the product of human creativity applied through a wide variety of arts and sciences as filters (known as secondary sources), archives house the raw data of history, the sources from which scholars create their own filtered narratives. Another way to look at it is to consider that a library is a place where a fact or a story can be found; an archives is a place where records, papers, manuscripts and other raw artifacts of knowledge can be found in their unbiased, original form. In addition to a strong public service motivation, archives serve a critical historical function of preserving the data from which scholarship might proceed again and again, regardless of the modes of thought of any particular historical moment. Thus the purpose of archives is to preserve the historical record of the society in which it functions. In this way, archives and records repositories, like libraries, serve a critical role in their social milieus, that of preserving and disseminating the collective knowledge of their cultures.

When we speak of archives and records management we really have in mind three distinct functions that all share a common goal, the preservation of source documents and artifacts of knowledge. An "archives" is a repository of the documents or other raw knowledge artifacts generated by a corporate body. Also, an archives might contain as well the personal papers of individuals. Records management utilizes the same set of principles as archives to help corporate entities manage their own working documents. A major difference between the two arises in the fact that while archivists work to preserve the raw data of history in specialized knowledge domains, records managers work for institutions to manage the crush of institutional records, many of which will be discarded.

Two principals underlie all archival functions, and both have to do with the context in which the preserved records were generated. These principals are called provenance, and original order. Provenance is the source of the documents or the records. It is considered critical to the perception of the contents of documents that they be maintained in the context in which they were generated. Likewise, the principal of original order dictates that the documents or records should be maintained in the order superimposed on them by the person or corporate entity that generated them. In the comprehension of these two principals lies the key distinction between the roles of archives and of libraries in society.

For instance, the records of an individual scholar might include letters to and from various other individuals, drafts of manuscripts of articles, books, speeches, lectures, etc., research data and statistical calculations, documents relevant to any professional organizations in which the individual has played a role, and so forth. Now, if we are able to sit down and peruse these documents altogether, then we are able to observe the progress of this individual's career, and perhaps even the generation of unique ideas and the path by which they evolved over the course of their successive promulgation. We might find, for instance, that a particular statistical observation is stated first on a sheet of note paper, then a bit later in an email or letter to a distant colleague, then perhaps initially in a lecture, before appearing in a more refined state in a journal article and years later being stated as a theory in a monograph. Had these documents not been maintained in a single collection, this observation might not have been possible, and the story of the generation of this particular theory might have been lost.

Thus it is apparent that understanding of historical methods is critical for archivists, and many earn degrees in history before taking coursework to become archivists. Archives, like libraries, are functional tools of the cultures in which they are situated. Institutional, regional, corporate, and national archives, as well as repositories of the records of individuals, all serve the purpose of historic preservation of artifacts that are intended to reach across time to continually service the search for knowledge. Archivists are functioning curators of truth in so far as they permit it to be interpreted and realized over and over through the evaluation of the resources they have acquired and preserved. Like librarians, archivists are service-oriented, and are very attuned to the potential uses of their collections. The profession of archivist has changed dramatically in recent years, particularly around the issues of preservation and description. Where at one time it was rare to find even a partial list of the contents of a collection, today archivists use a complex metadata structure called Encoded Archival Description (EAD) to create internet-accessible hyperlinked finding aids for their collections. This shift in emphasis has created distinct streams in archival careers, and helped lead to the shift from archivists with historical background alone, to a greater population of archivists with information science backgrounds as well.

The Society of American Archivists is a very powerful and influential professional society. SAA is not just a source of conferences and publications. Rather, it certifies its members academic qualifications, provides ongoing continuing education, and actively engages the development of new standards for professional performance. The SAA's defines archival work in these terms (http://www2.archivists. org/profession):

The primary task of the archivist is to establish and maintain control, both physical and intellectual, over records of enduring value; [and],
The work of the archivist is related to, but distinct from, that of certain other profession-als. The librarian and the archivist, for example, both collect, preserve, and make acces-sible materials for research; but significant differences exist in the way these materials are arranged, described, and used. The records manager and the archivist are also closely allied; however, the records manager controls vast quantities of institutional records, most of which will eventually be destroyed, while the archivist is concerned with relatively small quantities of records deemed important enough to be retained for an extended period. The museum curator and the archivist are associated; however, the museum curator collects, studies, and interprets mostly three-dimensional objects, while the archivist works with paper, film, and electronic records. Finally, the archivist and the historian have had a long-standing relationship; the archivist identifies, preserves, and makes the records accessible for use, while the historian uses archival records for research.

Whereas the American Library Association accredits schools that offer the pro-fessional degrees for librarianship, SAA does not accredit programs, but rather it certifies its members' qualifications. There are at least two educational paths for archivists: coursework in a department of history; or a masters in information stud-ies with a certificate in archival practice. Some schools offer specialized masters degrees in archival studies. Particular emphasis is placed on selection and acquisi-tion of archival materials, and arrangement and description of archival collections. Preservation is particularly critical for archivists, because the artifacts themselves are of as much value for history as any data they contain. The SAA directory of archival education lists thirty-nine programs leading to graduate degrees or certifi-cation in archival studies.

Regional, state provincial and other local associations of archivists exist all across North America. There are several national specialized associations of archi-vists in the United States, including the Academy of Certified Archivists (ACA), the Association of Moving Image Archivists (AMIA), and National Episcopal Histori-ans and Archivists.

A major census of archivists was undertaken in 2004 and the analysis of its re-sults indicated that the majority of archivists worked in academic institutions (36%) with the next largest group working for government (32%), and only small propor-tions working in private institutions. The majority of respondents described them-selves as archivists-manuscript curators (52.6%) with roughly 8% listed as manag-ers and another 6% as technical staff, indicating most archivists worked directly and intimately with collections (A*CENSUS 2006, p. 328). About 20% worked for historical societies, 30% for religious institutions, 17% for museums, and 12% for other non-profit institutions (A*CENSUS 2006, p. 345). Newer entrants to the field (41%) were more likely to have MLIS degrees; most had degrees in history as well (A*CENSUS 2006, p. 408).

Records managers also have a strong professional association, the Association of Records Managers and Administrators International (known as ARMA). Growing from the archival movement in the mid-twentieth century, records management de-veloped over the very real concern about the crush of current records in institutions and the likelihood many of them could not be maintained or even kept. Records management focuses on the life-cycle of records, including the systems designed for records-keeping, and recognizing the diverse motivations of the communities that generate and use these records. A good source for more detail about the development of both archives and records management is *The Archival Paradigm* (CLIR 2007).

4.2.3 Museums

Information professionals who work in museums have less of a structured profession, although the American Association of Museums is a primary advocacy, accreditation, and professional society. Museums are populated with archeologists, anthropologists, classicists, and scientists of all sorts for whom the acquisition and analysis of artifacts is a primary science. Curators, therefore, are more likely to be scientists engaged in the discovery of artifacts than they are to be information professionals. Museums have archivists whose job is to focus on the internal records of the museum, which themselves tell the story of the science that has generated the repository. There will also be conservationists and preservationists whose job it is to see that the artifacts are maintained and not allowed to deteriorate. The International Council of Museums offers this definition (http://www.aam-us.org/aboutmuseums/whatis.cfm) of a museum:

> A non-profitmaking, permanent institution in the service of society and of its development, and open to the public, which acquires, conserves, researches, communicates and exhibits, for purposes of study, education and enjoyment, material evidence of people and their environment.

"Museum studies" is a relatively new academic discipline, although (of course) museums have existed for thousands of years. A directory of programs maintained by the Smithsonian Institution (http://museumstudies.si.edu/courses.html) shows this diversity. Some programs are in schools of anthropology, some in schools of art, some are in museums themselves, and a few are now located in information schools. Often, these programs lead to a "certificate of museum practices," which, together with a doctorate in an associated discipline (anthropology, archeology, fine arts, etc.) provide the professional credentials for museum work.

Curatorial studies usually involve acquisition, exhibition, preservation, and cataloging of artifacts. Elective coursework runs the gamut from fund-raising, to ethnography, to the politics of museums, and even to how to create a new museum. To continue the theme of the information professional from the beginning of this chapter, museum curators also are curators of the truth, and yet it is their job to remain utterly objective as they stand apart from and alongside the collections of artifacts that constitute their charge. The job is more difficult than one might imagine, for it is impossible to know to what use an object might be put by a scholar. It is a standard of research that extant artifacts are biased by the fact of their survival, thus the museum curator's role is as much to interpret the collection as it is to gather it. Exhibits, and their catalogs, are just one part of the story to be told by a museum.

4.3 Organizations

Knowledge management is the largely corporate school of thought having to do with the means by which organizations create and govern their collective knowledge base. Knowledge management is a very recent development, dating its academic rise only to 1995, based on the conception that knowledge can be of two types—tacit and explicit—and that how an organization makes use of both is critical to the success of the organization. Academic work in knowledge management is focused on understanding the sources of knowledge, conflicting knowledge, competitive knowledge, and management information systems. Knowledge managers on the line in corporations work to establish intellectual capital, social networks, communities of practice, and tools for knowledge sharing. Taxonomies, or lists of terminology, and ontologies, or lists of concepts, are tools that are borrowed from the information science community and used in slightly different ways in knowledge management. Practices include knowledge audits, knowledge capture, and knowledge mapping.

Knowledge management is taught in schools of business and in information schools. Some have been so bold as to suggest that knowledge management might provide the long-sought umbrella discipline for librarianship (Chaudhry and Higgins 2001, p. 1). But for the most part, knowledge management is seen as a set of techniques for maximizing knowledge capital in organizations. A 2001 survey of courses offered found 30 of 37 were offered at the graduate level, spread more or less evenly among schools of business, computing and information (Chaudhry and Higgins 2001, p. 3). The major differences between traditional information studies and knowledge management include librarianship's focus on external sources (books, for example, and journals) rather than internalized knowledge and human capital, and of course, librarianship's traditional not-for-profit stance over against the competitive for-profit mode of the corporate environment (Ferguson et al. 2007). Librarians traditionally (except for special librarians, of course) are not working on the same wave-length as businesses when it comes to organizational goals. A professional association for knowledge management is maintained by a special interest group within the association for Information Science and Technology (ASIS&T SIG-KM). Closely allied with knowledge management is the area called information architecture, which is the collection of practices associated with management of digital information, especially that residing on the internet.

The role of knowledge managers and information architects is still a cultural role. Like their librarian counterparts, knowledge managers are involved in the dissemination of the culture of their organizations, and to a large extent also its preservation. Of course, the major difference is that knowledge managers work with humans to administer the capture and use of knowledge itself rather than a collection of artifacts that contain already synthesized external resources. Like their librarian counterparts, knowledge managers are involved in the objective dissemination of potential truth. The primary difference is simply alignment with corporate goals.

4.4   Information Professionals Are Gatekeepers

As we have seen the information process is central to the roles of all information professionals. Whether working as librarians, archivists, museum curators, knowledge managers or in any of the myriad other posts that fall within the embrace of information, it is facilitating the transfer of messages among humans for the purpose of allowing them to become informed that is the focus. We also have brought attention to other sorts of information organizations, such as indexing services, classifications, and even bibliographic utilities. All of these employ a mixture of librarians, knowledge managers, information technology specialists, computer scientists, and scholars of various stripes including specialists in knowledge organization. Their highly specialized staff members come from all of the domains described above and bring many of those professional talents to bear on the evolution and maintenance of their special, individual products. They, too, are gatekeepers.

In all cases, the cultural role of the institutions in which information professionals work is paramount—the information institutions are the collective memories of the cultures in which they reside. They exist not simply as dank repositories, but rather as very active and progressive partners in the information process. Information professionals serve to disseminate—which means not only to collect but also to distribute in a controlled manner—the knowledge that is the foundation of their culture. And here is the main point that draws all of these disparate professionals together—they all serve as gatekeepers in their cultures, deciding not only what knowledge is of high quality but also the means by which it is to be acquired, preserved, structured, managed, and made available for the process of becoming informed. It is a critical role for society at large that is played by the information professional.

References

A*CENSUS. 2006. Archival census and education needs survey in the United States. *American Archivist* 69:291–618.

Boulding, Kenneth. 1956. *The image: Knowledge in life and society*. Ann Arbor: University of Michigan Press.

Buckland, Michael K. 1988. *Library services in theory and context,* 2nd ed. Oxford: Pergamon Press.

Chaudhry, Abdus Sattar, and Susan Ellin Higgins. 2001. Perspectives on education for knowledge management. 67th IFLA Council and General Conference, 16–25 Aug 2001, Boston. http://hdl.handle.net/10150/106420. Accessed 14 April 2013.

Council on Library and Information Resources (CLIR). 2007. The archival paradigm: The genesis and rationales of archival principles and practices. http://www.clir.org/pubs/reports/pub89/archival.html. Accessed 14 April 2013.

Crawford, Walt, and Michael Gorman. 1995. *Future libraries: Dreams, madness, & reality*. Chicago: American Library Association.

Ferguson, Stuart, Mariam Sarrafzdeh, and Afsaneh Hazeri. 2007. Migrating LIS professionals into knowledge management roles: what are the barriers? *EDUCAUSE Australia 2007.*

Kuhn, Thomas. 1996. *The structure of scientific revolutions,* 3rd ed. Chicago: University of Chicago Press.

O'Donnell, James J. 1998. *Avatars of the word: From papyrus to cyberspace.* Cambridge: Harvard University Press.

Shera, Jesse H. 1976. *Introduction to library science: Basic elements of library service.* Littleton: Libraries Unlimited.

Chapter 5
Some History of Libraries, Library and Information Science, Information Technology

Abstract Information is a form of social capital, and information institutions of all sorts are disseminators of the cultures in which they arise. Therefore it is important also to understand the culture of the institutions themselves. Libraries, museums, archives, and repositories of knowledge artifacts have existed as long as societies have considered themselves organized. History demonstrates how such institutions have evolved from simple repositories to service providers. The introduction of scientific method applied to the problems of information service helped information workers move up a social ladder from custodians of artifacts to valued professionals. The evolution of ever more sophisticated information technologies accompanied the evolution of the discipline to the complex, interdisciplinary status it enjoys today.

5.1 Why Talk About History in This Way?

Like every other field of study it is important in our discipline for us to understand our roots, the better to understand the culture in which we operate. Our essential thesis is that information is a form of social capital, and that information institutions of all sorts (and especially libraries) are disseminators of the cultures in which they arise. This provides us with a sort of socio-cultural wrapper for our endeavor. But it is important also to understand the culture of the institutions themselves. Libraries, museums, archives, and repositories of knowledge artifacts have existed as long as societies have considered themselves organized—in other words forever. What, then, can we learn about the roles of libraries by looking at their history? We will see that such institutions have evolved from simple repositories to service providers. We will see how the introduction of scientific method applied to the problems of information service helped information workers move up a social ladder from custodians of artifacts to valued professionals. And we will see how the evolution of ever more sophisticated information technologies accompanied the evolution of the discipline to the complex, interdisciplinary status it enjoys today.

5.2 Some History of Libraries

Shera (1976, pp. 13–41) gives an overview of the history of libraries from Ancient times to the late twentieth century. We need to remember that society for much of its history was oral and not literate, by which we mean the society largely kept its stories current by telling them. Listeners memorized the stories and passed them on to new audiences. Libraries, or collections of documents, became important when theocratic societies developed the need for sacred texts as evidence. From the library at Karnak in 1200 B.C.E to the Dominican monasteries of 1200 C.E. this theme remains the prevalent cause for the development of libraries. So it is important to understand that the role of disseminator of culture was held primarily by the people themselves, the story-tellers. The role of the evidentiary library in a theocracy was to disseminate not so much the culture as the order of society. Highlights of this period are the ancient Greek libraries of the fifth century B.C.E., tended by public scribes and made open to scholars. The famous library at Alexandria was erected in about the third century B.C.E., and it contained not only books, but also specimens, artifacts, and art works; thus it was the central repository of the culture of its day. The collection of books (scrolls most likely) grew with the gustatory collecting of Ptolemy II, and the Alexandriana grew into the world's largest repository of human knowledge, including manuscripts from all of the known world.

From the renaissance onward in the western world libraries began to grow as repositories of knowledge, particularly as the church lost hegemony and the western world grew more secular. The invention of printing from movable type, attributed to Gutenberg in about 1450, was one of those moments in world history from which all that follows can be seen to have evolved, at least as far as the dissemination of knowledge is concerned. For it is from this moment that the cost of producing a book began to become affordable and the market for books became the catalyst for the invention of sophisticated indexes and catalogs. These tools in turn became catalysts for the development of larger libraries, mostly in educational institutions. The movement evolves right into the nineteenth century, through the enlightenment and into the development of increasingly democratic societies that were dependent on public education to produce an informed electorate. The rise of the ubiquitous public library as an educational institution took place as part of this movement on both sides of the Atlantic.

5.2.1 Librarianship in the U.S.

Librarianship in the United States was professionalized in the 1870s, primarily through efforts by Melville Dewey (1851–1931). Other than the Library of Congress, libraries that grew in the colonies were associated with what became educational institutions, such as Yale in New Haven or King's College (Columbia University) in New York. Public libraries really did begin with the unique initiative of Benjamin Franklin, who founded The Library Company of Philadelphia in 1731.

Dewey's developments took place in the period of Reconstruction after the Civil War, when education, industry, and the economy were all expanding rapidly, and automated printing technologies (and eventually the invention of paper made from wood pulp) led to an eventual "information explosion." Prior to this time librarianship had been custodial—librarians were the keepers of books. Now cheaper books were more plentiful, readership expanded dramatically as public education created a population of literate adults, the sciences and universities expanded as the industrial revolution gave way to modernity. Libraries became larger and more complex. It was through Dewey's initiative, together with other founding fathers of librarianship like Justin Winsor (1831–1897) and Charles Cutter (1837–1903), that librarianship in the United States grew into a valued service profession. Cutter especially was responsible for the codification of practices that still inform the construction of library catalogs today as tools for the discrete management of libraries and the knowledge they contained.

The American Library Association was formed in 1876 to provide an organization for the promotion and development of a profession. The first professional journal in the new field was the *American Library Journal* (today titled simply *Library Journal*). Thanks to Cutter's influence catalogs made information services possible. Reader and reference services were established and populated by the new cadre of librarians graduating from new professional schools. Dewey had opened the first school of "library economy" in 1887 and his graduates opened schools as they spread out across the country. Poole's first index to the contents of periodicals was also begun in this period. Justin Winsor (at Boston Public then later at Harvard), kept statistics of performance, kept annotated fiction lists, opened branches of the library, extended hours, and installed card catalogs that could be accessed by the general public. Both Dewey and Cutter created new library classification schemes that were intended to promote the browsing of book stacks. Interlibrary loan was introduced to allow libraries to supplement their contents. Winsor himself was among the first "scholar librarians" with technically able lieutenants, a pattern that still exists in the nation's academic libraries.

We also owe Dewey attribution for the feminization of the profession of librarianship. Dewey preferred the company of women and brought them into his school and thus into the professional ranks of librarianship, although in writing he clearly acknowledged their intellectual deficiencies. He rationalized that the low cost of women's pay was beneficial for the development of public institutions. By associating his new profession of librarianship with school teaching, which was seen as an appropriate role for women because it was closely associated with the concept of motherhood, Dewey attracted legions of women in search of careers to librarianship. By 1910 78 % of all librarians in the United States were women, and by 1920 the figure was 90 %. Until the late twentieth century this pattern persisted, with men serving in the roles of scholar librarian in the university libraries, but with women populating the ranks.

As noted, an important aspect of the growth of librarianship as a profession was the founding of professional societies. The founding of the American Library Association paralleled the founding of The Library Association (of Great Britain) in

1876, and the two nascent associations undertook several joint initiatives, including a joint code of cataloging rules issued in 1901. In 1909 the Special Libraries Association was founded as a utilitarian, information-oriented organization for mechanics and textile libraries, business-owned libraries, etc. In 1939 the Music Library Association (formerly a roundtable within ALA) formed its own separate professional society, generating a pattern for education and career paths. By World War II most of the profession had been established in the form in which it now exists.

5.3   The Evolution of Library and Information *Science*

Dewey founded the first professional school for the education of librarians, The School of Library Economy, opened at Columbia University in New York in 1887. The school was very successful, and when Dewey went to Albany to become director of the New York State Library in 1890 he took the school with him, where it continued to prosper. In 1923 a report by Charles Williamson, called "Training for Library Service" was issued suggesting the work of libraries be divided into professional and clerical positions. Professionals, or librarians, would be those with the knowledge of the principles of library service, and of the tools of bibliography, classification, cataloging, and information service. Librarians would be the managers and decision-makers; clerical staff would populate the technical offices of libraries. It would be the late twentieth century before this system was clearly codified in both libraries and educational institutions. But the die was cast and the nascent schools of librarianship began to rename themselves schools of library service and to cast off training for clerical roles. These schools offered bachelor's degrees in the 1920s, but soon would recast themselves (as did other professional schools) as graduate divisions in the universities.

Shortly thereafter the Carnegie Foundation offered the funds to endow a school that would offer only graduate degrees in librarianship, and in which the values of research as it was then understood in the sciences would be brought to bear on the problems of librarianship. The school was founded in 1926 at the University of Chicago with the name "The Graduate Library School." The name, which seems innocuous to us today, was of critical importance at the time to separate the school from its competitors who did not offer graduate degrees. Also, it was vital to place the school among the graduate divisions of the arts and sciences at Chicago. Almost simultaneously Dewey returned his school to Columbia University, now calling it "The School of Library Service" and now officially a graduate division of the university. From this point forward there was a movement across the United States to replace the former bachelor's degree in "library science" with the new masters degree, which now carried with it the values of research methods, as found in other sciences. Ironically, both the GLS and the SLS would be closed at almost the same time in the late 1980s.

We have already discussed the connotations of the various terms that describe our field. At this juncture we want to note the evolution from "library practice" and "library economy" to the term "library science." The term was first used in the 1930s and first appeared in two famous books that are foundational in the field. The first was S.R. Ranganathan's *The Five Laws of Library Science* (1931). This was a very exciting book, with an introduction by Berwick Sayers, then one of the most prominent librarians in England. The book's prefatory matter included breathless commentary about the rapid pace of scientific development in librarianship around the world. What better time for a set of "laws" to be promulgated for a new science. Hardly the stuff of logical positivism, Ranganathan's laws are rather humanistic in nature:

The first law: Books are for use.
The second law: Every reader his book.
The third law: Every book its reader.
The fourth law: Save the time of the reader.
The fifth law: The library is a growing organism.

But, to this day these five laws form the basis of library service around the world. It is easy to see how, insofar as they encapsulate the concepts of service—library use, circulation, document delivery, bibliographic efficiency, and adaptability—that were unknown prior to the professionalization of librarianship.

At the same time, Pierce Butler's 1933 *An Introduction to Library Science* laid out the positivist approach to the study of the problems of librarianship. Butler was a librarian by profession, but now was the professor of bibliographical history at the new GLS at Chicago. He brought to the table a discussion of the role of data collection by empirical observation and integrative evaluation leading to explanations of causality. These are the basic elements of the natural (and newly discovered at that time, the social) sciences. To this framework Butler added an enumeration of the problems central to librarianship, which were sociological (the social phenomena that propel the discovery of new knowledge), psychological (reading for pleasure, as an obsession, etc.), historical (bibliography as the history of the artifacts of knowledge), and practical (the management of libraries). Here we see the outline of today's curriculum in library and information science, to which has been added a large dose of technology in the form of information retrieval.

5.4 Some History of Information Technology

This simple narrative has moved rapidly from antiquity to the early twentieth century, from oral culture to literate, and from libraries as custodial repositories to libraries as institutions for the dissemination of knowledge. Libraries, archives, and museums were not differentiated institutions in the beginning. Likely they were undifferentiated collections of artifacts, special primarily for their provenance and associated with their creators and collectors. The artifacts were valued for many reasons, not necessarily for informative value in the way we understand it. During the rise of universities in the west in about the twelfth century, which happened as the canon law of western Christianity became increasingly codified, books became of value as tools in the defense of orthodoxy, and libraries as we now know them sprang up. Soon the art works, raw documents, and artifacts of antiquity migrated to their own institutions.

But by the late nineteenth century several people all had had the same idea, which was to incorporate all knowledge artifacts, and hence all knowledge as well, in a unified world catalog/index/encyclopedia to which everyone everywhere could have access. This idea has precedents all the way back to Aristotle, but some helpful landmarks begin with Denis Diderot (1713–1784) who envisioned a unified encyclopedia of all knowledge. In 1938 science fiction author H.G. Wells (1866–1946) wrote several essays about what he called the "World Brain." It was to be a digest of all human knowledge, and in particular it was intended to help scholars to synthesize disparate knowledge. He called it a "mental clearing house" for the mind.

We must consider in parallel the introduction of technology along the way, including great advances in printing technology. The twentieth century was to prove to be a time of major advances in bibliographical technology, especially reprography and automatic indexing, as well as computing. In the early part of the century, a movement born from the dreams of Belgian documentalist Paul Otlet and devoted to the recording of all human knowledge in a central repository led to the development of techniques such as microfilming, which were intended to make the content of brittle, valuable, or rare documents available worldwide for pennies. Digitization is the twenty-first century child of this movement, bringing us full texts online of many of the world's leading books.

Another major innovation of the twentieth century was born of the coincidence of a backlog of unindexed documents and the rapid escalation of global warfare. By the period of the second world war, science was advanced enough to create weapons of mass destruction, but bibliographical science had not yet achieved the ability to communicate essential research to scientists at distant points. The search for mechanical means of doing so led to the eventual employment of digital computers, which today are ubiquitous in information retrieval. By the 1960s (Rayward 1983) the reprography movement had merged with the information retrieval movement to evolve from its former position as "documentation" into what we now see as "information science." And, it had become apparent, following both the footsteps of Butler and Ranganathan, that librarianship was the technology that most closely adhered to the practice of information science. Thus the field began to change its name to "library-and-information science."

Two further contributions to information technology served as social catalysts for the technological age in which we now live. The first was the introduction of the dream of the Memex, by Vannevar Bush in 1945's *Atlantic Monthly*. Here was envisioned something like the microcomputer desktop of the end of the twentieth century, and perhaps the tablet or smart-phone of the near future—a single locus for a scholar in which he can find all knowledge that might be of importance to his work, and tools for synthesis as well. Bush had been part of the push to automate the retrieval of scientific information funded by what would become the National Science Foundation during the war (as had Frederick Kilgour, who in 1968 would found the OCLC international bibliographic utility). Of course, the idea of such a work station was not new, Otlet had envisioned something much like it even earlier. However, it was Bush's article that served as a catalyst in the popular press inspiring generations of scholars in computer and information sciences. Finally, we owe the realization of much of Bush and Otlet's dream to Tim Berners-Lee (1989), to whom often is attributed the creation of the World Wide Web.

References

Berners-Lee, Tim. 1989. Information management: A proposal. CERN. http://info.cern.ch/Proposal.html. Accessed 14 April 2013.

Bush, Vannevar. 1945. As we may think. *Atlantic Monthly* 176:101–108.

Ranganathan, Shiyali Ramramrita. 1931. *The five laws of library science*. Madras: Madras Library Association (London: Edward Goldston).

Rayward, W. Boyd. 1983. Librarianship and information research: Together or apart? In *The study of information: Interdisciplinary messages,* eds. Fritz Machlup and Una Mansfield, 399–405. New York: Wiley.

Shera, Jesse H. 1976. *Introduction to library science: Basic elements of library service*. Littleton: Libraries Unlimited.

Williamson, Charles C. 1923. *Training for library service: A report prepared for the Carnegie Corporation of New York*. New York: Updike.

Chapter 6
Gatekeepers: Information Dissemination

Abstract Information institutions are indeed repositories and information professionals are gatekeepers of those institutions. We need to think fully about the proper social role of institutions as disseminators of their cultures. To disseminate means to scatter, sow, spread and disperse; it depends on its obvious root which is a metaphor for "seed." The information process, which is our responsibility to disseminate, is a formalization of human inquisitiveness and socialization. The synergy of the role of information institutions lies in their responsibility to disseminate the nested and embedded cultures over which they have control. Publishers and producers of information objects play a critical role as well as gatekeepers by deciding what the market might bear. The information process must be ubiquitously made available in every occupied point in the culture, which must be permeated with its own seed, as it were, because the very survival of the culture demands it. A cultural moderating influence which is a sort of control mechanism erects boundaries that serve not only as limits but also as protective enclosures. Ethics codes guide professional practice. Concretizing forces and domain parameters aside, cultures require reinvention in order to thrive, and this requires a constant influx of new "seed," as it were. Dissemination of information, therefore, requires open access to knowledge.

6.1 On the Meaning of Dissemination

We have come to an understanding that information as an entity is the process of becoming informed, that information as a discipline is the domain in which that process is studied, and that information institutions exist as cultural entities with a social responsibility for the dissemination of their cultures. Along the way we have encountered a multiplicity of professional responsibilities that all serve to meet the challenges of the responsibility of preserving, protecting, and making available both the artifacts that are information objects and the process of becoming informed. We have a tendency to think of information institutions as grand repositories and of information professionals as keepers of the institutions. That tendency, honorable as it might be, keeps us from thinking fully about the proper social role of our institutions as disseminators of their cultures. In this essay I want to focus briefly on the full concept of dissemination.

R. P. Smiraglia, *Cultural Synergy in Information Institutions,*
DOI 10.1007/978-1-4939-1249-0_6, © Springer Science+Business Media New York 2014

The *Oxford English Dictionary Online* tells us that "disseminate" is a verb that means "to scatter abroad, as in sowing seed; to spread here and there; to disperse (things) so as to deposit them in all parts." The obvious root is a metaphor for seed; it means that which is to be scattered abroad is natural, endemic, inherent, and therefore of not only the institution but also of its culture. The information process, which is our responsibility to disseminate, is a formalization of very human inquisitiveness, on the one hand, and socialization, on the other. We desire to know and we desire to communicate what we know; the information process is a formalization of those desires, with highly detailed and sometimes complex heuristics. The process comes from within nested cultures and not just the externally visible culture, as, say, the Golda Meir Library at the University of Wisconsin, Milwaukee, disseminates the culture of the university, and that culture is nested within the culture of American academics, international scholarship, and Wisconsin as well. But also, embedded within the institution is its own institutional culture. All of these cultures are the institutions prerogative, indeed its responsibility, to disseminate.

I worked for 14 years as a music catalog librarian at the University of Illinois at Urbana-Champaign. I was young and energetic and the work was intellectually challenging. I loved music and reveled in the opportunity to live in a musical culture alongside performers, students, composers, musicologists and budding music educators. We sang answers to reference questions, we hummed at our desks as we engaged in the detective work of sifting through Gesamtausgabe and thematic catalogs to figure out just which "air" it was that had been "arranged" and wound up on our desk to be cataloged. At night I went to concerts or lectures or performed in orchestras, making a musical life into a rounded experience. It was an immense collection and therefore often it was possible to gather in one place all extant scores and parts of a given musical work, or of the works of a composer, and thus to see at a glance the physical artifacts representing the cultural power of that particular work or composer. It was evidence not only of the process of instantiation of a work, but also of the specifics of engraving, printing, reprinting, the commercial aspects of the performing industries, and so on. It gave me a very healthy respect for my predecessors who had acquired the collection and for our patrons in the musical community. What we did in the library found its way to listener's ears regularly and that seemed a profound responsibility. Still, my comprehension was from the inside of the library to the musical culture outside.

When I became a professor some years later and began a life of scholarship I became keenly aware of how dependent I was on good libraries. It was often a surprise to me to look in a library catalog and find what I needed, or to go to a shelf to browse and see not only what I had sought but related work collocated with it. My awareness shifted subtly as I realized this was possible only because great librarians had somehow imagined (I thought) what someone like me might need in a distant future and acquired it. It was a curious evolution in my thinking I suppose, because I should easily have understood that this was the other side of the proverbial coin. I should have seen that librarians working adeptly on the inside of the culture had made it possible for scholars to exploit the records of that culture to create new knowledge through research. Here is the other end of the process of dissemination, which is made possible because the culture is well and truly embraced by the information institution. In the 1980s I worked with archivists to help them embrace automation of their finding aids, first in the form of MARC records uploaded to RLIN or OCLC and later in the form of online web resources with EAD (Encoded Archival Description) metadata fueling their availability through search engines. Sometime in the early 2000s I began to work with cultural heritage experts on the CIDOC Conceptual Reference Model meta-ontology for information sharing, and about the same time I engaged in some fairly rigorous research at the University of Pennsylvania Museum of Archeology and Anthropology to uncover instantiation among the records of the artifacts in their collection. In the last several years as an active researcher in knowledge organization I have seen the work of editors and editorial boards of major classifications as they seek to comprehend not just the concepts in their schemes but also the depth of relationships inherent within the schemes and among the concepts and even among other relationships. In all of this I see the synergy of the role of information institutions to disseminate the nested and embedded cultures over which they have control.

I have alluded to publishing elsewhere among the essays in this book to explain the partnership among the culture's population, who create demand, and its information institutions, who manage the fulfillment of that demand. Publishers and producers of information objects play a critical role as well as gatekeepers by deciding what the market might bear. The contours of the print publishing industry are fairly visible at least among scholars. Writers write but publishers decide which writings might have buyers, and then they pay the costs of production to make those writings into publications that consumers can purchase. One of the laws of information is Lotka's Law of author productivity (Lotka 1926), which tells us that most authors only write one thing and only a small proportion of authors produce most of the writings available. Research on instantiation also has shown that this law predicts the proportion of works that will have multiple instantiations and even those that might have large networks of instantiations (Smiraglia 2001). Most authors only write one writing, and most writings are published only one time and that covers about sixty percent of all creative enterprise. For those cases scholars are dependent on the good judgment of librarians who acquire and preserve those writings for the rare future moment when they might be of importance to research. But for the remaining piece of the productivity pie, very few highly productive creators produce works that somehow grab the imagination of the cultures into which they are dispersed, and that acculturation acts as a catalyst for demand. New editions, translations, adaptations, screenplays, musical settings, and the proverbial lunchboxes and action figures are all the commercial products of this small cluster of very influential creators. Publishers and other commercial managers of information objects follow these demand curves and invest in the production and sale of these networks of instantiated ideas. This process likely is the expression of the thriving synergistic demand created in a culture that has had the information process fully disseminated within and throughout it. Instantiation along these lines is a sign that there is a continuing demand for information and the marketplace is meeting it. Sometimes gatekeeping works.

Scatter, sow, spread and disperse are all words that occur in the *OED online* definition I cited before. These are the verbs that give us the character of the job of information dissemination. The role of information institutions is not just to be repositories, and not just to make it possible to view an artifact or borrow a text or even to find a fact. Rather, the role is to make sure the information process is ubiquitously available in every corner, every nook and cranny, every occupied point in the culture. The culture must be permeated with its own seed, as it were, because the very survival of the culture demands it. The evolution and thriving of the culture depend on the dissemination of the information process. The gate swings both directions; gatekeepers open and close the gate, and consumers in a culture walk through the gate in both directions. A thriving culture is dependent on the gatekeeping function of its information institutions. This is the sum of their synergistic roles.

6.2   On Intellectual Freedom and the Right to Know

There is, in every culture, a moderating influence, a sort of control mechanism that might spring from a survival instinct. This means that every culture has boundaries and those boundaries serve not only as limits but also as protective enclosures. Collins (1998) has suggested knowledge domains ensure their own survival by concretizing when too many new ideas seem to be competing for demand, or else if they cannot concretize (perhaps by synthesizing some competing ideas) they split. It is a version of the idea put forward by Thomas Kuhn (1962) in his analysis of scientific paradigms. Domain analytic studies in knowledge organization (Smiraglia 2012 for example) show this effect repeatedly. A new domain springs up around an exciting idea, scholars and applications developers rush to explore and meet the demand, the culture begins to thrive and as it does so it grows exponentially. But the growth is also a threat to survival, so the culture's leaders (who likely are those creative people in the instantiating segment of the culture's ideas) erect boundaries, create organizational structures, and raise the intellectual bar to keep the domain's points of view to a manageable number. If this works the culture thrives and persists; if not, the culture breaks apart, and new exciting ideas become the genesis of new knowledge cultures.

Something like this happens in society as well, and when it does ideas are sometimes imperiled. Censorship looms as one group with real or imagined control decides which ideas can or cannot be disseminated as representative of the culture at large. Human history is replete with examples and there is no need to recite them here. Information institutions are gatekeepers with a responsibility for disseminating the culture and that means they sometimes run up against these concretizing impulses as well. It is a potentially dangerous shoal for them to navigate.

In the United States libraries adhere to a code of ethics that demands they preserve the public's right to know, and this means there is an institutional commitment to open access to the information process, especially among public libraries. Here is the text of the American Library Association's Code of Ethics (ALA 2008):

As members of the American Library Association, we recognize the importance of codifying and making known to the profession and to the general public the ethical principles that guide the work of librarians, other professionals providing information services, library trustees and library staffs.

Ethical dilemmas occur when values are in conflict. The American Library Association Code of Ethics states the values to which we are committed, and embodies the ethical responsibilities of the profession in this changing information environment.

We significantly influence or control the selection, organization, preservation, and dissemination of information. In a political system grounded in an informed citizenry, we are members of a profession explicitly committed to intellectual freedom and the freedom of access to information. We have a special obligation to ensure the free flow of information and ideas to present and future generations.

The principles of this Code are expressed in broad statements to guide ethical decision making. These statements provide a framework; they cannot and do not dictate conduct to cover particular situations.

1. We provide the highest level of service to all library users through appropriate and usefully organized resources; equitable service policies; equitable access; and accurate, unbiased, and courteous responses to all requests.
2. We uphold the principles of intellectual freedom and resist all efforts to censor library resources.
3. We protect each library user's right to privacy and confidentiality with respect to information sought or received and resources consulted, borrowed, acquired or transmitted.
4. We respect intellectual property rights and advocate balance between the interests of information users and rights holders.
5. We treat co-workers and other colleagues with respect, fairness, and good faith, and advocate conditions of employment that safeguard the rights and welfare of all employees of our institutions.
6. We do not advance private interests at the expense of library users, colleagues, or our employing institutions.
7. We distinguish between our personal convictions and professional duties and do not allow our personal beliefs to interfere with fair representation of the aims of our institutions or the provision of access to their information resources.
8. We strive for excellence in the profession by maintaining and enhancing our own knowledge and skills, by encouraging the professional development of co-workers, and by fostering the aspirations of potential members of the profession.

Adopted at the 1939 Midwinter Meeting by the ALA Council; amended June 30, 1981; June 28, 1995; and January 22, 2008.

Other kinds of information institutions, including archives and libraries in private institutions, must adhere to various economic or institutional restrictions on who might use their resources. It is not really a form of censorship, per se, but it does throw up gates (not barriers, per se, so much as guidance mechanisms) around the public's right to know. Institutions with these kinds of parameters have a responsibility to engage in consortia for information sharing. Similarly, institutions whose job is to preserve or conserve precious artifacts must, of course, do just that by restricting access. Here is the code of ethics of the Society of American Archivists (2012):

Archives are created by a wide array of groups and provide evidence of the full range of human experience. Archivists endeavor to ensure that those materials, entrusted to their care, will be accessible over time as evidence of human activity and social organization. Archivists embrace principles that foster the transparency of their actions and that inspire confidence in the profession. A distinct body of ethical norms helps archivists navigate the complex situations and issues that can arise in the course of their work.

The Society of American Archivists is a membership organization comprising individuals and organizations dedicated to the selection, care, preservation, and administration of historical and documentary records of enduring value for the benefit of current and future generations.

The Society endorses this Code of Ethics for Archivists as principles of the profession. This Code should be read in conjunction with SAA's "Core Values of Archivists." Together they provide guidance to archivists and increase awareness of ethical concerns among archivists, their colleagues, and the rest of society. As advocates for documentary collections and cultural objects under their care, archivists aspire to carry out their professional activities with the highest standard of professional conduct. The behaviors and characteristics outlined in this Code of Ethics should serve as aspirational principles for archivists to consider as they strive to create trusted archival institutions.

Professional Relationships: Archivists cooperate and collaborate with other archivists, and respect them and their institutions' missions and collecting policies. In their professional relationships with donors, records creators, users, and colleagues, archivists are honest, fair, collegial, and equitable.

Judgment: Archivists exercise professional judgment in appraising, acquiring, and processing materials to ensure the preservation, authenticity, diversity, and lasting cultural and historical value of their collections. Archivists should carefully document their collections-related decisions and activities to make their role in the selection, retention, or creation of the historical record transparent to their institutions, donors, and users. Archivists are encouraged to consult with colleagues, relevant professionals, and communities of interest to ensure that diverse perspectives inform their actions and decisions.

Authenticity: Archivists ensure the authenticity and continuing usability of records in their care. They document and protect the unique archival characteristics of records and strive to protect the records' intellectual and physical integrity from tampering or corruption. Archivists may not willfully alter, manipulate, or destroy data or records to conceal facts or distort evidence. They thoroughly document any actions that may cause changes to the records in their care or raise questions about the records' authenticity.

Security and Protection: Archivists protect all documentary materials for which they are responsible. They take steps to minimize the natural physical deterioration of records and implement specific security policies to protect digital records. Archivists guard all records against accidental damage, vandalism, and theft and have well-formulated plans in place to respond to any disasters that may threaten records. Archivists cooperate actively with colleagues and law enforcement agencies to apprehend and prosecute vandals and thieves.

Access and Use: Recognizing that use is the fundamental reason for keeping archives, archivists actively promote open and equitable access to the records in their care within the context of their institutions' missions and their intended user groups. They minimize restrictions and maximize ease of access. They facilitate the continuing accessibility and intelligibility of archival materials in all formats. Archivists formulate and disseminate institutional access policies along with strategies that encourage responsible use. They work with donors and originating agencies to ensure that any restrictions are appropriate, well-documented, and equitably enforced. When repositories require restrictions to protect confidential and proprietary information, such restrictions should be implemented in an impartial manner. In all questions of access, archivists seek practical solutions that balance competing principles and interests.

Privacy: Archivists recognize that privacy is sanctioned by law. They establish procedures and policies to protect the interests of the donors, individuals, groups, and institutions whose public and private lives and activities are recorded in their holdings. As appropriate, archivists place access restrictions on collections to ensure that privacy and confidentiality are maintained, particularly for individuals and groups who have no voice or role in collections' creation, retention, or public use. Archivists promote the respectful use of culturally sensitive materials in their care by encouraging researchers to consult with communities of origin, recognizing that privacy has both legal and cultural dimensions. Archivists respect all users' rights to privacy by maintaining the confidentiality of their research and protecting any personal information collected about the users in accordance with their institutions' policies.

Trust: Archivists should not take unfair advantage of their privileged access to and control of historical records and documentary materials. They execute their work knowing that they must ensure proper custody for the documents and records entrusted to them. Archivists should demonstrate professional integrity and avoid potential conflicts of interest. They strive to balance the sometimes-competing interests of all stakeholders.

Responsible use of documents and the public's right to know must be balanced, carefully, with the responsibility to protect the artifacts as well as the privacy of their creators. Cultural sensitivity, to both the documents and their originating sources, plays a crucial role in the archivist's approach to information dissemination.

The International Council of Museums similarly maintains a detailed code of ethics for museums. The document is too long to display here in its entirety, but we can take space to consider its very informative table of contents, which is in essence the outline of the code (ICOM 2013) together with principles stated at the opening of each section:

1. Museums preserve, interpret and promote the natural and cultural inheritance of humanity.

   Principle: Museums are responsible for the tangible and intangible natural and cultural heritage. Governing bodies and those concerned with the strategic direction and oversight of museums have a primary responsibility to protect and promote this heritage as well as the human, physical and financial resources made available for that purpose.

   – Institutional standing
   – Physical resources
   – Financial resources
   – Personnel

2. Museums that maintain collections hold them in trust for the benefit of society and its development.

   Principle: Museums have the duty to acquire, preserve and promote their collections as a contribution to safeguarding the natural, cultural and scientific heritage. Their collections are a significant public inheritance, have a special position in law and are protected by international legislation. Inherent in this public trust is the notion of stewardship that includes rightful ownership, permanence, documentation, accessibility and responsible disposal.

   – Acquiring collections
   – Removing collections
   – Care of collections

3. Museums hold primary evidence for establishing and furthering knowledge.
   Principle: Museums have particular responsibilities to all for the care, accessibility and interpretation of primary evidence collected and held in their collections.

   - Primary evidence
   - Museum collecting & research

4. Museums provide opportunities for the appreciation, understanding and management of the natural and cultural heritage.
   Principle: Museums have an important duty to develop their educational role and attract wider audiences from the community, locality, or group they serve. Interaction with the constituent community and promotion of their heritage is an integral part of the educational role of the museum.

   - Display and exhibition
   - Other resources

5. Museums hold resources that provide opportunities for other public services and benefits.
   Principle: Museums utilise a wide variety of specialisms, skills and physical resources that have a far broader application than in the museum. This may lead to shared resources or the provision of services as an extension of the museum's activities. These should be organised in such a way that they do not compromise the museum's stated mission.

   - Identification services

6. Museums work in close collaboration with the communities from which their collections originate as well as those they serve.
   Principle: Museum collections reflect the cultural and natural heritage of the communities from which they have been derived. As such, they have a character beyond that of ordinary property, which may include strong affinities with national, regional, local, ethnic, religious or political identity. It is important therefore that museum policy is responsive to this situation.

   - Origin of collections
   - Respect for communities served

7. Museums operate in a legal manner.
   Principle: Museums must conform fully to international, regional, national and local legislation and treaty obligations. In addition, the governing body should comply with any legally binding trusts or conditions relating to any aspect of the museum, its collections and operations.

   - Legal framework

8. Museums operate in a professional manner.
   Principle: Members of the museum profession should observe accepted standards and laws and uphold the dignity and honour of their profession. They

should safeguard the public against illegal or unethical professional conduct. Every opportunity should be used to inform and educate the public about the aims, purposes, and aspirations of the profession to develop a better public understanding of the contributions of museums to society.

- Professional conduct
- Conflicts of interest

The ICOM code of ethics makes it clear that the dissemination of cultural heritage is the primary communicative, or informative, priority of museums. That priority must be balanced with the responsibilities to preserve, promote, and share the collections, and to generate constant educational use of the precious contents. In this way it is possible to maintain that responsibility while still engaging in widespread information dissemination. Many museums today make their collections accessible outside the walls of the museum through digital representations. This is one example of allowing the gate to swing in both directions.

Concretizing forces and domain parameters aside, cultures require reinvention in order to thrive, and this requires a constant influx of new "seed," as it were. Dissemination of information, therefore, requires open access to knowledge, ready access to the processes of information, and preservation of everyone's right to know. The synergy of information institutions demands their hearty participation in maintaining gates that swing in both directions.

References

American Library Association. 2008. Code of ethics. http://www.ala.org/advocacy/proethics/code-ofethics/codeethics. Accessed 3 April 2014.

Collins, Randall. 1998. *The sociology of philosophies: A global theory of intellectual change.* Cambridge: Belknap.

International Council of Museums. 2013. ICOM Code of ethics for museums. http://icom.museum/the-vision/code-of-ethics/introduction/#sommairecontent. Accessed 3 April 2014.

Kuhn, Thomas. 1962. *The structure of scientific revolutions.* Chicago: University of Chicago Press.

Lotka, Alfred J. 1926. The frequency distribution of scientific productivity. *Journal of the Washington Academy of Sciences* 16:317–323.

Smiraglia, Richard P. 2001. Further progress on theory in knowledge organization. *Canadian Journal of Information and Library Science* 26:30–49.

Smiraglia, Richard P. 2012. Epistemology of domain analysis. In *Cultural frames of knowledge,* eds. R. P. Smiraglia and H. Lee, 111–124. Würzburg: Ergon.

Society of American Archivists. 2012. Code of ethics for archivists. http://www2.archivists.org/statements/saa-core-values-statement-and-code-of-ethics. Accessed 3 April 2014.

Chapter 7
Knowledge Organization: Bibliography as Synergic Catalyst

Abstract Knowledge organization is the field of inquiry wherein is studied the nature and order of knowledge that underlies all applications in information. Navigating natural orders, and creating and imposing useful orders, are the province of the domain of knowledge organization. Bibliographic control is an application of knowledge organization in which professionals "control" the arrangement of certain artifacts and their intellectual content for retrieval. Resource description, subject headings and classification are the tools of bibliography exercised especially by information institutions under the rubric of bibliographic control. Not only is a bibliographic record a form of synergic control, the professional culture that maintains the languages and techniques are themselves synergic. Bias is potentially everywhere, yet professional ethics require our institutions to resist it at any cost. An open question remains about what institutions are to do to bridge the gap between bibliographic control and imposing social bias. Another open question is whether more than one ontology (classification) could be applied simultaneously in a virtual catalog. Visualization of knowledge organization systems and components can provide useful navigational maps. From library and museum catalogs to medical and supermarket classifications, knowledge organization systems drive social behavior in every part of human endeavor. And for that reason, the effects of social epistemology can be both beneficial and deleterious. The synergy lies in the concept of cultural warrant.

7.1 Organization is a Powerful Cultural Tool

The way a society sees to its own internal order is a powerful reflection of the society's norms. Take, for example, the way in which streets are laid out. In colonial Philadelphia, streets fit between houses built before automobiles were invented. Residents frequently curse visiting drivers for driving down the center of a two-lane street. But, of course, to the visitor from suburbia, it looks about as wide as a single lane. Now consider a street in Amsterdam, with separate (and visibly distinct) lanes for automobiles, trams and buses, bicycles, and pedestrians. It says something in each case about the priorities of the culture.

Of course this also is true of the order of knowledge, and the manner in which the records of knowledge are organized and made available for retrieval in information institutions. If an information institution is seen as primarily engaged in cultural dissemination, then how many of its decisions about the order of knowledge will directly reflect the values of that culture? In this chapter I look at the general structure of knowledge organization in information institutions, particularly in libraries, but also in social applications. I consider how this synergic knowledge organization structure is a reflection of cultures—both social and institutional. From library and museum catalogs to medical and supermarket classifications, knowledge organization systems drive social behavior in every part of human endeavor. And for that reason, the effects of social epistemology can be both beneficial and deleterious. Social epistemology is carried out in a major way through what is called bibliographic control.

7.2　Knowledge Organization, Bibliographic Control

Knowledge organization (also known as KO) is the field of inquiry (often but not exclusively thought of as situated within information) where the nature and order of knowledge is studied. It underlies all applications in information as a discipline and as a profession. It might seem obvious to say that nothing can be retrieved without some sense of the order in which it has been arranged, yet the application of knowledge organization is not so obvious. Everything from the human genome to your local supermarket provides an example of ordered knowledge that must be accessed, yet for which the order might not be readily apparent. Navigating natural orders, and creating and imposing useful orders, are the province of the domain of knowledge organization.

Knowledge organization is also an activity or a set of techniques. Some or most of these techniques are referred to in the practical world as bibliographic control. We use the generic term knowledge organization to embrace information artifacts other than books, and also to embrace activities in knowledge organization outside the realm of librarianship, such as in archives and records management, museum management, information retrieval, knowledge management, etc., as well as the classification of research findings in the sciences.

Bibliographic control is an application of knowledge organization in which professionals (the librarians, archivists, curators, knowledge managers, etc.) "control" the arrangement of certain artifacts (documents, books, journals, maps, sound, film, etc.) and their intellectual content for retrieval. The purpose of bibliographic control is to allow users to "control" retrieval of necessary information. We can consider bibliographic control as a process in which bibliographic data (like indexes and catalog records) are created, manipulated, and made ready for retrieval. Bibliographic data are elements such as titles, names, and subject words that can be found on artifacts of recorded knowledge (book spines, title pages, movie title screens, etc.). These data naturally occur on the artifacts, that is, they are inherent.

Such bibliographic data can be controlled to make a resource accessible to users. We do this by transcribing these data in a formalized way into bibliographic records

Fig. 7.1 Dublin Core metadata record from OCLC WorldCat

found in catalogs. The data, once transcribed, allow us to create a "surrogate" for the item, that can then be used in several different ways—we can designate all of its parts as indexable so a user can find and display the single bibliographic record under the title, the author, the publisher, by date, or by series, or by topic. By creating a bibliographic record we allow ourselves a lot of leeway for manipulating bibliographic data. Traditionally such records were used to make up catalogs, but more recently the data components have become known as metadata, which, when resident in a Web resource (usually in its otherwise invisible header) are used by search engines for retrieval. Here is an illustration from the OCLC WorldCat of a simple bibliographic record display from a library catalog alongside the same data in Dublin Core Metadata form (Fig. 7.1):

It is easy enough to see how complex even a simple bibliographic description can become. The instructions for recording descriptive metadata and for generating subject descriptors, name identifiers, and classification symbols are also complex; Svenonius (2000) suggested that the rules themselves constitute discrete languages. Although we can imagine it to be a fairly simple task to index recorded knowledge, in fact, large and complicated interwoven sets of such languages are required. Not only is a bibliographic record a form of synergic control, the professional culture that maintains the languages and techniques are themselves synergic.

Fig. 7.2 Query process

user   response

7.3   Collection-based Information Retrieval

The result is a highly specialized information retrieval system; one that supports only collection-based (usually bibliographic) data. (Other information retrieval systems have different foci—your dentist probably has a database of his patients and his suppliers, your supermarket probably has a database of products, etc.). Information retrieval systems can be seen as intermediaries between a susceptible user and the solution to a problem (Buckland 1988, p. 82). For example, a susceptible user is a person who has a question of some sort—what time is the flight to Cancun, where can I find a certain light fixture, how much does a garage door cost?—we say the user is susceptible because there is an information gap in this person that creates a sort of challenging, inquisitive psychological state. The information-storage-and-retrieval (ISAR) system can be thought of as a sort of magic box to which the user will put a query. (Soon we will see that there is nothing magic about it, but at the moment a susceptible user approaches it there might as well be.) On the other side of the system is the solution to the problem—the flight departs at 1:30, the store on King Street has lighting, a garage door costs about $ 1200. Here is a model (Fig. 7.2):

Many things can go wrong in this model, and they often do. For example, if I ask about "wall sconces," but the database has only the term "lighting" there will not be a match. If I ask about flights to Cancun but the system has only "departures" listed there will not be a match. Or, if I ask about garage doors, the system might reply with the prices of thousands of doors—from French doors to garden gates (this is information overload). The essential problem for information retrieval, then, is translation, and a critical aspect of translation is noise reduction. We want the system to retrieve only that which is exactly relevant to our query—no more and no less, but we also want it to retrieve everything that is relevant to our query. The proportion of data retrieved that are relevant is called "precision," and the proportion of all relevant data in the system that is retrieved is called "recall." Science has shown that there is an inverse relation between recall and precision—the higher the recall the lower the precision and vice versa. Again, the essence of the problem is translation.

So we can either create a specific vocabulary and tell the user "use only these terms to query the system" or we can teach the system to translate a user's query into the language used in the system. At the end of the model we have the same problem—the recall must either be translated into the user's language, or the user must translate it. There are many solutions to this problem in information retrieval, but the most important for us are what are called knowledge organization systems (KOS), thesauri and classifications.

I've alluded to "noise" twice, and noise is simply irrelevant material that gets in the way. For instance, if I want the address of the Toronto restaurant Hair of the Dog I can put that phrase into a search engine. But the response I get likely will include the Irish band with the same name—noise—information that looks right but is not. Again, there are many solutions to this problem in information retrieval, but KOS are used often to reduce noise by limiting the terminology in a system.

7.4   Collection-based Information Retrieval Systems

Collection-based retrieval systems (such as library or museum catalogs), then, are the tools of knowledge organization used as internal mechanisms for order. Bibliographies, of course, are a kind of bibliographic retrieval system. Compiled by scholars working alone in highly concentrated areas of study, bibliographies represent the judgment of a peer-reviewed group of scholars about the literature they collectively consider to be seminal.

The two main kinds of bibliographic retrieval systems are indexes and catalogs. An index is a system that contains bibliographic data about an entire literature—for example, the index *Library Literature & Information Science Index Full Text (EBSCO)* contains citations to journal articles (and pointers to their texts) in the field of information studies. Search engines on the Web are essentially indexes of the Internet. A catalog is a system that contains bibliographic data about a particular local collection of documents, usually the contents of a library. Bibliographic utilities exist that are "union" catalogs that incorporate data about collections in many libraries all merged into a single database. OCLC's WorldCat is an example.

7.5   Functions of Bibliographic Systems

Regardless whether we are talking about an index or a catalog, all such bibliographic information retrieval systems must satisfy three functions. These have been developed over centuries and are found to be universally applicable. The functions are called (1) finding, (2) collocating, and (3) evaluating. The finding function is sometimes also called the identifying function. This means that a user with a citation ought to be able to find that particular item in the system. If I ask for Harry Potter, I either ought to find Harry Potter or I ought to be told there is none in the system. This function is the most straightforward and it supports what is called known-item searching. Unfortunately, most searching is not known-item searching, but involves hunting. This requires things to be gathered together in useful ways so a searcher can evaluate clusters or related material. Imagine you want a can of soup, and you go to the supermarket, but you discover the entire store is just arranged according to when boxes were received. You either have to take the first can of soup you come across, or you have to walk around the entire store looking at every product present to make a choice. Libraries are similar—if we did not use KOS to organize bibliographic data you would have to read every book to figure out which one you needed. So we gather things according to names, titles, subjects, and sometimes even just alphabetically. This allows more sophisticated navigation. You don't have to look through books about pottery to find Harry Potter. This is called the "collocating" function, and sometimes is also called the gathering function. To "collocate" is literally to co-locate—to place things side by side. The final function is the most important and is called the evaluating function. This means the system has to have enough information to allow the searcher to make an informed choice. What if you want to read Harry Potter, and the system tells you it has Harry Potter on shelf 17, but when you get there you find Harry Potter dolls instead of books (or even videos)? You would have wasted your time with a false positive. So the system must say "I have 3 Harry Potter books and 2 Harry Potter movies, which do you want?"

Subject headings are terms that come from a controlled vocabulary (often the *Library of Congress Subject Headings*) that are used to index the topic of a resource. Classification serves the same purpose, but it uses symbols—usually letters and numbers—to represent topics, which allows related subjects to be grouped together regardless of the linguistic variations in their names. For instance, golden delicious and Macintosh are both kinds of apples, but if we describe them using language one goes under "g" (for golden delicious), one under "m" (for Macintosh), and neither falls under "a" (for apples). But with a simple classification

A Apples
AG Golden delicious
AM Macintosh

we can cause all apples to be found in one sequence, at the same time we can designate specific types. This is called a hierarchy and it is the most basic kind of classification. Notice too that the classification consists of symbolic notation and term designations.

All of this together—resource description, subject headings and classification—are the tools of bibliography exercised especially by information institutions under the rubric of bibliographic control. You can see that many decisions must be made daily about how to structure knowledge, and especially about how to categorize and group entities. One of the problems is that this activity is highly judgmental, which leads to decisions that either facilitate or obscure retrieval.

7.6 The Effect of *Control*

Sometimes standard bibliographic control has been used inferentially (or, often, less subtly) to organize knowledge in culturally acceptable modes. Social epistemology means information institutions disseminate their own cultures, but sometimes this leads to negative synergies. I begin with Olson's (2001a) review of the so-called "universality of naming" from the point of view of feminist-deconstruction. For example, subject headings are based on a concept called "unity," meaning "select the term most people use." Olson shows how this "rule" can be used to select "mankind" instead of "people," "man" instead of "men and women," and so forth—if in the context of a given culture universality really represents the hegemony of the more powerful party. Women are marginalized in most societies, and that is reflected in the subject headings and classifications used in libraries. We have the subject headings "Doctors" and "Women doctors." What does that say about our cultural biases? Olson (2004) also used a similar approach to demonstrate the mob mentality of both subject headings and classifications used in libraries. She described the power of hierarchy as a form of hegemony that insists on the subordination of terminology. Looking for apples? You'd better know the botanical class in which they appear if you expect to find them. Similarly, the equation of terms as "same" or "different" represents a value judgment. Olson (2001b) suggested that classification gathers things according to commonalities that represent the biased judgments of culture. Folk literature, for example, is not the same as literature—the latter being a fine art, and the former being a form of linguistic exercise.

The current instantiation of Dewey's classification comes under significant criticism because of the way in which it forces knowledge to be organized according to the cultural norms of white, male, western society. Olson (1998) demonstrated the denigration of women, Puerto Ricans, Chinese-, Japanese-, and Mexican-Americans, Jews, Native Americans, the entire developing world, gays, teenagers, seniors, people with disabilities—none of them fared well in Dewey's classification. Why? Because their marginalization is reflected in the literature that is collected deliberately by information institutions, such as the Library of Congress, who hold authority over the dissemination of knowledge throughout American culture. This is reflected in the Dewey classification, because the rule of literary warrant insists that only knowledge held in books collected by libraries may be included, and it must be included in a way that reflects the opinion of the authors of the books involved. Does this sound like a circular argument? Yes, of course. But so does most social discrimination—"you cannot be equal, because heretofore you never have been"—or "we've always done it this way."

Furner (2007) used critical race theory to demonstrate how Dewey could be deracialized, offering for the first time a workable solution to a more egalitarian classification. He wrote (2007, p. 165):

> We might consider that any decision taken to prevent classifiers and searchers from the use of racial categories is to ignore an everyday reality in which those categories are invoked not only in the distribution of social and political power, but also in individuals' self-identification.

Although, bias has its cultural role, as Hjørland pointed out (2008) in describing the cultural influence of the placement of concepts in classification. His best example? The Canary Islands briefly belonged to Denmark. In Danish libraries, they are classified as part of Denmark. Is that bias? Or is it cultural collocation for Danish library users?

7.7 The Power of a Category

Anytime you have ever been singled out from the crowd you have experienced the power of discrimination. And every time you have been a part of a group—say, airline passengers who have to remove their shoes to go through security—who has been assigned a deleterious role in society, you have paid for your membership with harsh treatment. The same is true of the ways in which libraries and museums and archives create arrangements of resources for users. Bias is potentially everywhere, yet professional ethics require our institutions to resist it at any cost. What, then, are institutions to do about the standard practices they employ—subject headings and classifications—that reflect centuries-old biases? This remains an open question, as does the question of whether more than one ontology (classification) could be applied simultaneously in a virtual catalog. Is it possible that Danes and Canary Islanders could both have their way?

7.8 What of Objects and Everyday Things?

We make a mistake when we think that knowledge organization is about classification and that makes it about books in libraries. Knowledge organization is used the world over, as Bowker and Star (1999) so eloquently detailed, to order everything from medical decisions to insurance payments to racial profiles. There is a reason, as I frequently tell my students, that you have trouble finding stoned-wheat thins in the supermarket—often they are not on the shelves with other kinds of crackers because they are made in Canada, which makes them international. It is a simple example of the consequence of a market-based otherwise pragmatic classification. Bowker and Star detail some of the more nefarious consequences of missing diagnoses or strict racial segregation under apartheid.

In the last several years the phenomenon of the "social" Web has arisen, allowing everyone to "tag" all kinds of web resources. Individual users of resources can add descriptive terms as a kind of personal indexing system. This practice has sometimes been called "folksonomy," because it generates a kind of folk taxonomy. Research has shown that despite the egalitarian dreams of web designers, individuals tag rather for their own benefit (Kipp 2008; Smiraglia 2010). And because everyday humans are involved in this form of everyday classification (Jacob 2001), problems and biases creep in (Keilty 2009). Social epistemology is applicable here as well, even in the unorganized folksonomic arena. The tags are a form of cultural dissemination—meaning both curation and indexing for retrieval—and they permit a kind of multi-cultural synergy. However, taggers also demonstrate definitively that they adhere to a kind of bandwagon effect in which the tagged resources and the tags themselves both constitute a form of social capital (Smiraglia 2012a); leaders tags become the focal points or bandwagons that draw followers, resulting in the imposition of culturally-held biases.

7.9   What if There Were a Map?

Bibliographic structures can be conceived of in abstract form and perceived as network structures. In fact, an important aspect of the traditional catalog has been what we call it's "syndetic structure," or the network of connections among entities that form navigable pathways. Traditionally these structural elements were invisible, or visible only in part, through explicit references such as "see also" or "see the narrower term." Here is a simple example of terms related to banking. If we form the terms into an alphabetical list and then accompany each term with a list of terms related to it (NT is narrower term; BT is broader term; RT is related term) we get a thesaurus.

Banks
NT Deposits
NT Investments
NT Loans

Business [loans]
BT Loans

Deposits
BT Banks
RT Investments
RT Loans

Home equity [mortgage]
BT Mortgage

Investments
BT Banks
RT Deposits
RT Loans

Loans
BT Banks
RT Deposits
RT Investments
NT Business
NT Personal
NT Mortgage

Mortgage [loans]
BT Loans
NT Home equity
NT Purchase
NT Vacation residence

Purchase [mortgage]
BT Mortgage

Vacation residence [mortgage]
BT Mortgage

The list is helpful for organizing terminology, but its real application comes when it is used to index knowledge for retrieval. And if we reorganize the terms into a visualization demonstrating all of the relationships we get something quite like a map of the domain.

Now we can see easily how to move from one point in the domain to another along specific pathways. This is a simple example, but the application of informetric techniques has raised some intriguing possibilities for introducing navigable visualizations into what used to be simple bibliographic control.

In knowledge organization as a domain of study an explicit form of informetrics is referred to as "domain analysis." Domain analysis is the study of a discipline, or discourse community, to comprehend and capture its vocabulary, which in turn is a representation of its ontology. From this we can begin to generate knowledge organization systems that explicitly offer control to the members of the group, or domain. Smiraglia (2012b) reviewed a large variety of such studies ranging from citation analyses of all sorts to ethnographic research with hobbyists. Several kinds of visualizations of domain knowledge are possible, and often these are called maps to the domain. For example, an international symposium was held in 2013 on classification and visualization by the Universal Decimal Classification Consortium, in October in The Hague, Netherlands. There were 22 carefully selected papers presented at this symposium, and one could easily think of the assembled participants as a sort of domain. To understand what discourse took place at the symposium we might enter the titles of the papers into a visualization tool (in this case the Voyant Tool: Reveal your Text at http://voyant-tools.org) to produce a "map" of the major themes.

From the map we learn that "visualization," "knowledge," and "classification" were the most frequently used terms, but we also see that those dense clusters are surrounded by more granular terminology, helping form the context. Here we see terms such as "interfaces" and "cultural" and "information" and "collections" but also smaller terms such as "modeling" and "taxonomy" and even "multiverse." The major terms form the boundaries of the shared knowledge of this simple domain, but the granular terms help fill in our understanding of the context of the symposium.

An interesting idea has arisen concerning what might happen if a search beginning from a known work of interest were conducted by tracing subject headings assigned to similar books. The result of a preliminary research project (Gabel and Smiraglia 2009) was a sort of subject map of a domain, which shows not just the simple subject of the book itself, but also neighboring concepts. Here is a "map" from that study:

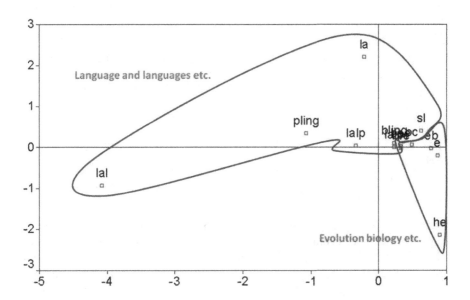

In this example, the search began with a book about the origin of languages, but as you can see, many "neighbors" were discovered. Here is a list of those terms, which were abbreviated for the map:

LCSH	Abbreviation
Behavior evolution	Bee
Biolinguistics	Bling
Brain—Evolution	Bre
Cognition and culture	Cac
Evolution	E
Evolution (Biology)	Eb
Human beings—Origin	Hbo
Human evolution	He
Linguistics	L
Language acquisition	La
Language and languages	Lal
Language and languages—Origin	Lalo
Language and languages—Philosophy	Lalp
Neuropsychology	N
Natural selection	Ns
Psychology	P
Psychology, Comparative	Pc
Psycholinguistics	Pling
Sign language	Sl

What we see in the map is that there are two "neighborhoods"—"language and languages etc." and "evolution biology etc." Within those two clusters reside works on psycholinguistics, cognition, and biolinguistics. The map tells us that not only does our original work lie in the proximity of other works about language and languages, but also in relative proximity to clusters of works on evolution, cognition, and the role of language in human evolution. This map is a two-dimensional representation of a three-dimensional statistical procedure (in this case produced with IBM-SPSS™ that is essentially a visualization of proximity in the co-assignment of subject headings by catalogers in the bibliographic environment of the OCLC WorldCat. It is a bit clunky as a visualization because it is designed to explicate research results in a scientific paper. What if we could make an actual map of these relationships?

A network map is a kind of visualization that can demonstrate connected relationships in a data set, or among concepts in a domain. Here is a network map created from the same data used above using an open-source software tool called Gephi:

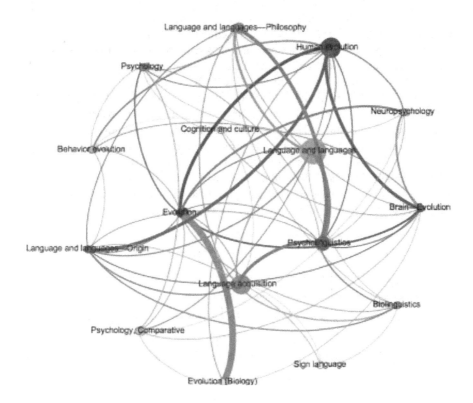

Now we see not only the two clusters "language and languages" and "evolution biology" represented with the different colors, but also we see the direct pathways among associated concepts. "Language acquisition" is on the road from "Psycholinguistics" but is rather distant from "cognition and culture," although that route can now be easily negotiated as well. Network maps like this could help searchers visualize quickly how to navigate a large and linguistically diverse collection, thus increasing the power of the searcher even in densely populated bibliographic files.

Of course, the future is already upon us. Complex ontologies are being created to provide better ways to map resources and to provide more meaningful pathways among them. Never mind the simple syndetic structure of subject headings—these tools will allow never before comprehensible connections to be made by scholars.

Imagine you are looking at a statue in a museum and notice it has a gouge in it. You look in the catalog and learn it was hit by a piece of a meteor. You can hyperlink to a description of the meteor in a library, or to a piece of the same meteor in a museum in another part of the world, from which you can link to a geological analysis of its chemical composition, and an astronomical analysis of its origin and trajectory. Information institutions will become more alike as they are once again perceived as repositories with similar missions—the dissemination of information.

One such promising ontology was developed by the museum community for information sharing about cultural heritage, but now has grown exponentially. It is the object-oriented empirically-based CIDOC *Conceptual Reference Model* (CIDOC-*CRM*). (International Council of Museums, International Committee for Documentation. 2011) Essential entities are "persistent items," "places," "actors," "appellations," and "stuff." The original model has been mapped to a large number of other conceptual models to promote information-sharing, including the library-based *Functional Requirements for Bibliographic Data* (FRBR) and the archives-based *Encoded Archival Description*, as well as the very simple and generic *Dublin Core Metadata Set*. Here is an illustration from the *CRM* website showing the core ontology conformed to Dublin Core (http://www.cidoc-crm.org/).

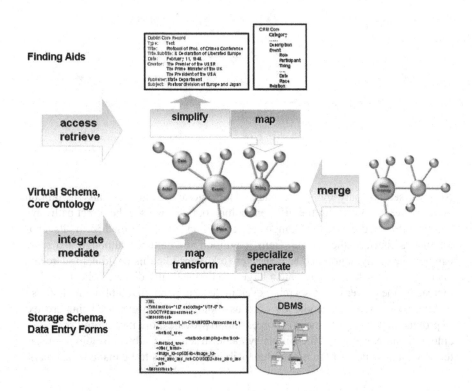

The original model has been mapped to a large number of other conceptual models to promote information-sharing, including the library-based *Functional Requirements for Bibliographic Data* and the archives-based *Encoded Archival Description*, as well as the very simple and generic *Dublin Core Metadata Set*. Here is another illustration showing how the core ontology has been aligned with the bibliographic model from *FRBR*.

Merging the core ontology CIDOC CRM (ISO21127) with FRBR

With ontologies such as this it will be possible to map everything in order to promote true information dissemination by bringing together as yet undiscovered related knowledge entities.

7.10   The Synergy Relies on Cultural Warrant

Knowledge organization should be seen as a synergic catalyst in all of its varied forms. From library and museum catalogs to medical and supermarket classifications, knowledge organization systems drive social behavior in every part of human endeavor. And for that reason, the effects of social epistemology can be both beneficial and deleterious. Despite the benefit derived from having a ubiquitous bibliographic classification like Dewey's facilitating browsing in public libraries, we must be aware of how the human impulse to classify can lead to negative synergies as well as positive.

Recent conferences focused on the ethics of knowledge organization have relied on the notion of cultural warrant (Beghtol 2005) as a starting point for ethical decision-making. In two conferences held in Milwaukee in 2009 and 2012, participants raised issues critical for ethical research and development in knowledge organization. The main themes from 2009 are shown in this diagram:

The user was clearly the most important aspect for ethical decision-making, in research and in the evolution of knowledge organization systems of all sorts. A similar but more refined set of themes emerged in 2012:

The emphasis on ethical representation of knowledge to help people shows the importance of the comprehension of cultural warrant in the evolution of knowledge organization as a synergistic component of the process of disseminating information across society.

In other words, it is not just that a domain has a specific ontology or vocabulary, but rather, it is critical to comprehend the cultural context for that ontology or vocabulary. To use the power of categories to create cultural discrimination or to support cultural oppression is unethical. The enshrine such oppressive cultural forces in knowledge organization systems is to make them subsidiary agents in the role of social epistemology in the empowerment of information dissemination. In other words, bibliography, knowledge organization and informetrics are pivotal synergic catalysts.

References

Beghtol, Clare. 2005. Ethical decision-making for knowledge representation and organization systems for global use. *Journal of the American Society for Information Science and Technology* 56:903–912.

Bowker, Geoffrey C., and Susan Leigh Star. 1999. *Sorting things out: classification and its consequences*. Cambridge: MIT.

Buckland, Michael K. 1988. *Library services in theory and context*. 2nd ed. New York: Pergamon.

Furner, Jonathan. 2007. Dewey deracialized: A critical race-theoretic perspective. *Knowledge Organization* 34:144–168.

Gabel, Jeff, and Richard P. Smiraglia. 2009. Visualizing similarity in subject term co-assignment. In Breitenstein, Micki and Loschko, Cheryl Lin, eds., Bridging Worlds, Connecting People: Classification Transcending Boundaries—Proceedings of the 20th SIG/Classification Research Workshop, November 7, 2009. http://www.journals.lib.washington.edu/index.php/acro/article/view/12886/11382.

Hjørland, Birger. 2008. Deliberate bias in knowledge organization? In Clément Arsenault and Joseph T. Tennis eds., *Culture and identity in knowledge organization: Proceedings of the Tenth International ISKO Conference 5–8 August 2008 Montréal, Canada.* Würzburg: Ergon-Verlag, 254–261.

International Council of Museums, and International Committee for Documentation. 2011. Definition of the CIDOC conceptual reference model, version 5.0.4. http://www.cidoc-crm.org/official_release_cidoc.html.

Jacob, Elin K. 2001. The everyday world of work: Two approaches to the investigation of classification in context. *Journal of Documentation* 57:76–99.

Keilty, Patrick. 2009. Tabulating queer: Space, perversion, and belonging. *Knowledge Organization* 36:240–248.

Kipp, Margaret E. I. 2008. @toread and cool: subjective, affective and associative factors in tagging. In Catherine Guastavino and James Turner eds., *Proceedings of the 36th annual conference of the Canadian Association for Information Science (CAIS), University of British Columbia, Vancouver, June 5–7, 2008.* http://www.cais-acsi.ca/proceedings/2008/kipp_2008.pdf.

Olson, Hope A. 1998. Mapping beyond Dewey's boundaries: constructing classificatory space for marginalized knowledge domains. *Library Trends* 47 (2): 233–254.

Olson, Hope A. 2001a. Patriarchal structures of subject access and subversive techniques for change. *Canadian Journal of Information and Library Science* 26:1–29.

Olson, Hope A. 2001b. Sameness and difference: a cultural foundation of classification. *Library Resources & Technical Services* 45:115–122.

Olson, Hope A. 2004. The ubiquitous hierarchy: An army to overcome the threat of a mob. *Library Trends* 52 (3): 604–616.

Smiraglia, Richard P. 2010. Self-reflection, perception, cognitive semantics: How social is social tagging? In: Elaine Ménard and Valerie Nesset eds., *Information Science: Synergy through Diversity, Proceedings of the 38th Annual CAIS/ACSI Conference, Concordia University, Montreal, Quebec. June 2–4 2010*. http://www.cais-acsi.ca/proceedings/2010/CAIS055_Smiraglia_Final.pdf.

Smiraglia, Richard P. 2012a. Jumping on the Bandwagon: Visualizing the Social Space of Social Taggers. In Annabel Quaan-Haase, Victoria L. Rubin, and Debbie Chaves eds. Information in a local and global context: Proceedings of the 40th Annual Conference of the Canadian Association for Information Science, Wilfred Laurier University/University of Waterloo, Waterloo Ontario, May 31–June 2, 2012. http://www.cais-acsi.ca/conf_proceedings_2012.htm.

Smiraglia, Richard P. 2012b. Epistemology of domain analysis. In *Cultural frames of knowledge,* eds. Richard P. Smiraglia and Lee Hur-Li, 111–124. Würzburg: Ergon.

Svenonius, Elaine. 2000. *The intellectual foundation of information organization*. Cambridge: MIT.

Chapter 8
Into the Future Boldly: The Imperative for Cultural Synergy

Abstract The various components that comprise the information domain possess the potential synergistic forces to yield a more powerful institutional culture of and for information. This synergistic outcome I wish to call the Virtual Information Scape. One synergistic effect that could be provided by a virtual information scape would be the ability to cluster cultural indicators across, or through, or among information objects regardless of institution of residence, language, or any other partial imposed boundary barrier. Another synergy is a cross- and meta-institutional approach to information-sharing. The information-sharing in which we engage is our cultural capital. A third synergy must come from re-envisioning the information domain such that we curate domains of research across institutional boundaries. A fourth synergy emerges from the development of core ethical standards for information. We live on the cusp of a virtual world, interactivity is the essential link, virtual space is social space.

Synergy occurs when the collective power of combined forces stimulates the evolution of a greater entity that is more than the sum of its prior parts. In this series of essays I have tried to demonstrate the potential synergistic effect of cultural synergy of information institutions. That is, I have analyzed the basic forces that constitute and govern the missions of information institutions, the information objects they collect, their collective information missions, and the cultures from which they arise. The point of this exercise is to bring us to the hopeful conclusion that the various components that comprise the information domain possess the potential synergistic forces to yield a more powerful institutional culture of and for information. This synergistic outcome I wish to call the Virtual Information Scape. Toward a description of this future virtual reality, contribute the outcomes of the essays that comprise this volume. With these we have learned:

- Information institutions are disseminators of their cultures, and thus represent a rich quilt of interwoven patches including dimensions of topical and cultural trajectories, as well as information processes. These intersecting lines of cultural mission are trajectories for synergy—interconnecting and evolving the collectivity of information institutions through the building up of humankind's knowledge base and capacity for information-sharing.

R. P. Smiraglia, *Cultural Synergy in Information Institutions,*
DOI 10.1007/978-1-4939-1249-0_8, © Springer Science+Business Media New York 2014

- Information is knowledge perceived, and therefore the process of becoming in-formed—neither the data nor the vehicle, neither the fact nor the document, but rather the process of sharing and perceiving the fruits of recorded knowledge.
- The information domain is a meta-discipline that has evolved from the conver-gence of library and information science with other components of cognitive sci-ence. Our research crosses disciplinary boundaries, synthesizing knowledge as it goes. There is a small base of theoretical knowledge into the essential properties of information (the process) and its carriers (knowledge artifacts and systems that organize and provide access to them), as well as a shared base of principles that inform the information professions.
- The information process is central to the roles of all information professionals, facilitating the transfer of messages among humans for the purpose of allow-ing them to become informed. In all cases, the cultural role of the institution is paramount serving as collective memory. Information professionals serve to dis-seminate—not only to collect but also to distribute in a controlled manner—the knowledge that is the foundation of their culture. They all serve as gatekeepers in their cultures, deciding not only what knowledge is of high quality but also the means by which it is to be acquired, preserved, structured, managed, and made available for the process of becoming informed.
- Information is a form of social capital such that information institutions of all sorts are disseminators of the cultures in which they arise. The socio-cultural implication is that over time and across cultures information institutions have evolved from simple repositories to service providers promoting the sharing of information processes.
- Society's norms are powerfully reflected in the orders it imposes and in the man-ners in which its knowledge base is recorded, organized, and made available. The same is true of the powerful grip of cultures. Thus the ordering of knowl-edge is a powerful tool of social epistemology.

Ergo, there is already synergy among information institutions. What greater synergy could be accomplished with deliberate attention to the intercallation of synergistic forces? The answer emerges from analysis of the three synergies that emerge from these essays.

8.1   Synergies

8.1.1   Synergy 1: Information Objects as Cultural Artifacts

Every information institution of every type has at its center a collection of informa-tion objects. These information objects are all, also, cultural artifacts. Thus, one synergistic effect that could be provided by a virtual information scape would be the ability to cluster cultural indicators across, or through, or among information objects regardless of institution of residence, language, or any other partial imposed boundary barrier. Metadata systems are at present too object-specific to accommodate such an enterprise, focusing instead in each case on the physical and collection-specific details of information objects. But information-sharing ontologies such as the CIDOC Conceptual Reference Model (http://www.cidoc-crm.org/) exist in which event-based indicators once encoded become identifiable cultural indicators that could, through data-mining and clustering operations, provide cultural synergy.

8.1.2 Synergy 2: Information Process as Cultural Action

We already have seen that "information"—the primary artifactual property of information institutions is, in fact, a process. Furthermore, we have seen that because the social epistemology of our ethos dictates our missions as disseminators (in all of its guises) of information, which is a process, that we have in fact another synergy present in our cross- and meta-institutional approach to information-sharing. In fact, the extent to which we share information is a measure of our cultural capital. Or, more directly stated, the information-sharing in which we engage is our cultural capital. This is an area for synergistic action across information institutions.

Here we can appeal to ideas like those of Bourdieu, whose work points to an understanding of metaphorical social space, a sort of perceived community notion of territoriality. Social space is any space where humans interact. Real places such as supermarkets and train stations constitute visible and obvious social spaces. But social space also can be metaphorical, when it describes the perceived territoriality of human existence. The idea is that humans perceive themselves against a backdrop of experience, which can be grasped metaphorically using a spatial, or proto-geographical, template. Distance and closeness within social space are perceived spatially but filtered functionally through degrees of intimacy, power, etc. It is this second, metaphorical, meaning that is often used to describe communal or community activity in Web 2.0 social applications.

A particularly effective interpretation of social space is described by Bourdieu (1991). As context he proposes the social world as topological (229), constructed on basic principles of "differentiation or distribution constituted by the set of properties active … [which are] able to confer force or power." Actors in social space are defined by their relative positions as well as by their interactions (230). Actors may occupy only one region but are distributed in two dimensions, which are circumscribed by the volume of capital they possess and the composition of their capital (231). Song (2010, p. 267) made reference to Bourdieu when she suggests a shift from Web 1.0 to Web 2.0 that took place in the second dimension as capital shifted from non-economic social poles to predominantly for-profit economic poles. North et al. (2008, p. 897) placed young people in the social space of Web 2.0 according to the first dimension, according to the volume of their cultural capital. Nascimento and Marteleto (2008, p. 400) suggested the perception of actors in Web 2.0 was key to their own realization of how they occupy social space, in other words, self-reflection is an essential component of how they use their social capital.

Budd (2003, p. 29) referred to Bourdieu while looking toward a cultural warrant for social classification that embraces as definitive the "differences and distinctions" that bring people into classes—their social capital—and therefore views resources as discursive acts.

Information institutions, which after all are populated and run by humans, are participants in the game of interterritoriality. That is, these institutions and their staffs view themselves as occupying a protogeographical space alongside the real geographical space. Thus the Rijksmuseum in Amsterdam is, in fact, the Royal Netherlands Art Museum, and it is in fact a Dutch museum in The Netherlands. But it is also a western European repository of art that stands over and against the art held in other museums in Europe, which themselves are culturally diverse from museums elsewhere in the world.

The virtual information scape calls on all information institutions to use these multiple information spaces as synergistic territories across which shifting information capital in the form of information sharing can be used as a more powerful distributive information force, a sort of super information supply-chain.

8.1.3   Synergy 3: Cross- or Meta-Institutional Curation

Here we come to the most radical if perhaps also most conservative of my proposals, and that is that we must re-envision the information domain such that we curate domains of research across institutional boundaries. We saw in the discussion of dissemination how gatekeeping requires consortial participation on the part of information institutions. We saw in the discussion of knowledge organization how the synergic action of data and knowledge control can lead to searching and knowledge acquisition across institutional boundaries.

It is am imperative of the Virtual Information Scape that information institutions create channels for working together that also allow cross and meta-institutional research. This will require cross- and meta-institutional curation. The virtual knowledge scape represented by the Semantic Web is a beginning, because it allows us to learn where related entities might be extant. But it is hardly enough. Information institutions need to take responsibility for curation across their own geoterrestrial boundaries. I am asking not just for cooperation, but for deliberate integration of curation.

Much can be accomplished using data-mining, of course. If all information institutions made all of their content available in digital form, it would be possible to *impose* cross-institutional curation through the evolution of meta-institutional data-mining agencies. Perhaps this brings us full circle back to the dreams of Paul Otlet. But it is certainly possible to use the digital footprints created by encoding with a meta-ontology like the CIDOC CRM to classify unknown but related knowledge entities encapsulated in knowledge objects (see Zherebchevsky et al. 2008). Applications, such as the proposed "idea collider" (Smiraglia and van den Heuvel 2011) can be used similarly to extract not only semantic matches but also syntactic matches within recorded knowledge. Together with other bold applications, information as a discipline and information institutions as its engines can point the way to an interconnected synergistic future in which knowledge that now is hidden is unlocked, shared, and inculcated.

8.1.4 Synergy 4: Core Ethical Standards for Information

The entire information process is at the center of the dissemination of culture, and it is for that reason that information institutions arise and play a critical role. Without the institutions the culture would be at risk. On the other hand, without dedicated information professionals, the risk of concretization might imperil the evolution of culture. The two risks are a creative opportunity for information as a process, providing a dichotomous tension in the action of information dissemination to preserve a culture even as we nurture its evolution. For this reason, information requires a core set of ethical standards.

Such a core can emerge from the synergy of already existing professional information standards. Key elements are clear:

- Preserve, interpret, promote: information dissemination requires a balance between preservation of core artifacts and comprehension of the essential need to see that they are used appropriately. This includes assuring the authenticity of artifacts, as well as providing equitable access to a variety of interpretations of their content. Primary and secondary evidence are held in trust for the benefit of the culture. Tools for extracting data must be generated at the highest level of efficacy both to ensure the preservation of the evidence and to guarantee its dissemination.
- Intellectual freedom requires open and equitable access to evidence held in information institutions. This includes the requirement that tools for knowledge organization be developed free of cultural biases that might impair access to any group of users.
- Intellectual property rights are primary for the continued evolution of the culture, therefore these rights must be upheld and protected by information institutions.
- The informed public must be protected from private interests. Information institutions serve the culture at large and must maintain the highest standards across the board if conflicting demands arise between the needs of government or commercial interests and the needs of the public.
- The privacy of donors must be respected. If information dissemination begins with acquisition of primary evidence it is essential that the pool of future accessions is as fulsome as possible. Therefore it is critical to create equitable policies that protect the lives of donors whose records or possessions become the evidence in information repositories.
- Uphold the dignity of the institution and its professionals. Information professionals and the institutions in which they operate must be above reproach in order to properly engage their cultural mission of dissemination. This requires

professional cooperation, collaboration across institutional boundaries, and maintaining the highest level of trust with donors, collectors, and users of information artifacts.

In this as in other aspects of cultural synergy we can build on a solid core of ethics that already exist and are promulgated by existing institutions and professions. What is required for the synergy is cross- and meta-institutional and professional collaboration. We must see that while intellectual freedom demands access to all potential knowledge, appropriate restrictions that balance the privacy of sources are required. At the same time, the public, which is the culture, must be uppermost in the prioritization of demands on the synergized system of information dissemination.

8.2   Conclusion: The Virtual Information Scape

Of course, in some ways we already are there. We already can envision the virtual information scape. Instead of silos, or marble buildings, it looks rather like this (Fig. 8.1):

This is a knowledge map created in Amsterdam's Knowledge Space Lab, which was an experimental space within the Virtual Knowledge Studio, a research group that was devoted to disseminating virtual knowledge as an information process (those are my words, based on my experience as a visitor and associate of the VKS and its successor research group; the VKS's fellows might have put it differently). Virtual knowledge is knowledge that is known and held collectively in the world's metaphorical hands as digital information. The process of becoming informed takes place (or can take place) in a virtual reality in which all knowledge is digitized and the information process must serve as the data-mining collocating device. Virtual knowledge is connected knowledge.

The large spherical representations in the illustration are visualizations of the connectedness of knowledge in Wikipedia and the Universal Decimal Classification. This is just one possible visualization of the Virtual Information Scape. Everything is connected to everything else, all that remains is for us to find the pathways for navigating the networked knowledge of our fast evolving virtual world. How do we get there from here? The answer is complex. The truth is we are well en route. For example, the World Digital Library (http://www.wdl.org/en/) is just one iteration of the imminent future. The literature of information science is replete with research on the specifics of maximizing the potential of this semantic web.

The fact is, we live on the cusp of that virtual world, near the border between the richly mechanized modernity of the twentieth century and the virtual post-modernity of the twenty-first, where humans, now untethered from encumbrances such as hard-wired telephones, televisions and desktop computers reside instead in the

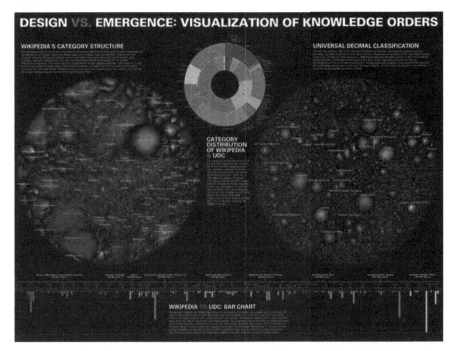

Fig. 8.1 Map of knowledge orders (Salah et al. 2011)

virtual world of Web 2.0 apps. Open an Uber™ app and a car service comes to your door in most of the world's major cities; take a photo out your office window and Facebook makes it available for your friends on the other side of the world to "like." "Virtual knowledge" is the social capital of the twenty-first century, embedded in digital infrastructures and with the potential for radical change in all realms of human activity from engineering to medicine, from art to travel, from research to the narrative of history (Wouters et al. 2013, p. 11 ff.).

Of course, interactivity is the essential link that makes Web 2.0 social applications into virtual spaces. Virtual space is social space, because it is where people interact, whether it is perceived metaphorically as merely territorial or whether it takes on the trappings of proto-geographical space. People interacting in virtual space maintain varying degrees of interdependence, which can be perceived as closeness or distance, metaphorically. Closeness is a sign of dependence, or of social collaboration, distance is a mark of independence, and sometimes is a sign of leadership. Observing the real interactions taking place in virtual space is one way of visualizing the exchange of information. The Virtual Information Scape is here, it is our responsibility to recognize it and nurture its evolution into a world replete with information sharing of our collective virtual knowledge.

References

Bourdieu, Pierre. 1991. *Language & symbolic power*. Cambridge: Harvard University Press. (edited and introduced by John B. Thompson, translated by Gino Raymond and Matthew Adamson).

Budd, John. 2003. Library, praxis, and symbolic power. *Library Quarterly* 73:19–32.

Nascimento, Denise Morado, and Regina Maria Marteleto. 2008. Social field, domains of knowledge and informational practice. *Journal of Documentation* 64:397–412.

North, Sue, Ilana Snyder, and Scott Bulfin. 2008. Digital tastes: Social class and young people's technology use. *Information, Communication & Society* 11:895–911.

Salah, Alkim Almila Akdag, Cheng Gao, Andrea Scharnhorst, and Krzysztof Suchecki. 2011. *Design vs. emergence: Visualisation of knowledge orders*. Courtesy of The Knowledge Space Lab, Royal Netherlands Academy of Arts and Sciences. In "7th Iteration (2011): Science Maps as Visual Interfaces to Digital Libraries," *Places & spaces: Mapping science*, edited by Katy Börner and Michael J. Stamper. http://scimaps.org/maps/map/design_vs_emergence__127/.

Smiraglia, Richard P. and Charles van den Heuvel. 2011. Idea Collider: from a theory of knowledge organization to a theory of knowledge interaction. Bulletin of the American Society for Information Science and Technology 37 no. 4:43–47.

Song, Felicia Wu. 2010. Theorizing Web 2.0. *Information, Communication & Society* 13:249–275.

Wouters, Paul, Anne Beaulieu, Andrea Scharnhorst, and Sally Wyatt, eds. 2013. *Virtual knowledge: Experimenting in the humanities and the social sciences*. Cambridge: MIT Press.

Zherebchevsky, Sergey, Nicolette Ceo, Michiko Tanaka, David Jank, Richard Smiraglia, and Stephen Stead. 2008. Mining maps of information objects: An exploratory ontological excursion. Poster at American Society for Information Science and Technology Annual Meeting, Columbus Ohio, 24 October 2008.

Printed in the United States
By Bookmasters